70 X 7

FORGIVING YOUR ABUSERS

SCOTT GREEN

CONTENTS

DEDICATIONS

To my beautiful wife, Suzanne,

> My best friend and soulmate. I love you more than you'll ever know. Thank you for loving and supporting me through my journey of forgiveness.

To my two beautiful daughters, Jessi and Victoria,

> Thank you for loving me in spite of my insecurities and dysfunctions, and for supporting me along this difficult journey. I love you both so much.

NOTE TO READERS

While *70 x 7* is a book about forgiveness based upon God's word, it also includes my personal experience as a victim of abuse. This story contains physical child abuse, emotional abuse, and non-explicit sexual abuse. Additionally, in telling an honest and faithful account of my experience, I use occasional mild language when quoting my abusers. The subject matter and content might not be suitable for all readers. Some names, locations, and identifying characteristics have been changed to protect the privacy of those depicted.

-Scott Green

PREFACE

I sat in the sanctuary with my eyes fixed on the charismatic Pastor, tuned into every word as he preached out of Matthew 18. *"Then Peter came to Jesus and asked, 'Lord, how many times shall I forgive my brother or sister who sins against me? Up to seven times?' Jesus answered, ' I tell you, not seven times, but seventy times seven.' " (Matthew 18:21-22)*

At that moment, my heart skipped a beat, and everything else he said afterward became white noise in the background. My mind raced to comprehend what the Pastor had just read. *"...not seven times, but seventy times seven."* The phrase continued to echo in my head, *"Seventy times seven, seventy times seven..."*

I've read that before; I already knew this. It's a familiar scripture I've taught others, but today that phrase hit me harder than ever.

My thoughts flooded to specific individuals in my past who have sinned against me through physical and sexual abuse.

Suddenly, I wanted to stand up and scream in response,

"But, Pastor, you don't know what these people did to me, not just once, but repeatedly! You don't know how much pain they inflicted on me or how hard I struggled to overcome the emotional wounds. I suffered for years under their abuse, and I still carry the scars of those wounds in my heart. I can never get back what these people stole from me. They deserve to suffer as much as I have. How can I forgive that? How can you stand there and honestly expect me to forgive them? It's not that simple! I can't do it!"

I sat there with these thoughts and emotions running through my mind as the hot tears rolled down my cheek. I wiped them away quickly, looking around to see if anyone noticed I was crying.

The Pastor continued his sermon out of Matthew. *"Then the master called the servant in. 'You wicked servant,' he said, 'I canceled all that debt of yours because you begged me to. Shouldn't you have had mercy on your fellow servant as I had on you?' In anger, his master handed him over to the jailers to be tortured until he could pay back all he owed."*

The Pastor became very silent and raised his head from his notes. He took off his glasses and lowered his voice. *"This is how my heavenly Father will treat each of you unless you forgive your brother or sister from your heart."* (Matthew *18:32-35)*

My body went numb, and my heart sank into my chest. I heard nothing else that morning from the sermon. Those last few words haunted me, over and over, like a terrible song you can't shake out of your head. *"This is how my heavenly Father will treat each of you unless you forgive your brother or sister from your heart."*

Now, I'm no stranger to the Word of God. I've been a Christian for over 30 years and graduated from discipleship classes and Bible school. I was a youth pastor for seven years. I ministered in several positions of authority within the church, including pastoring a small church in Mississippi for 13 years.

This passage is something I have preached on several times, so why did this passage of scripture hit me so hard emotionally this morning? Why was it suddenly haunting me today like a heavy conviction of sin?

The Holy Spirit immediately answered me as if he had heard my questions. "You still carry the pain and the poison of unforgiveness in your heart."

"How? I already dealt with this. Lord, I gave this to you years ago." And then there was a silence.

"Didn't I, Lord? At least, I thought I did." More silence.

"If I did, why does it still hurt so much?" The tears flowed as I realized I was still suffering from the pain of my abuse and unforgiveness for my abusers.

INTRODUCTION

Recovering from the pain of abuse and offense is a much more common struggle among Christians than I would like to admit. We may seem like we have it all together on the outside as we smile and go to church, greet one another with hugs and pleasantries, and actively participate in worship. Still, on the inside, we are hiding some painful scars from our past.

We have unseen wounds inflicted upon us through hateful or hurtful acts of injustice, abuse, lies, broken trust, and deceit. No one can see the level of emotional damage we are experiencing. All it takes is for one memory to resurface or one act committed by someone to trigger and peel back that hidden emotional scar. Suddenly, out of nowhere, it hurts all over again because we never treated the wound appropriately. We cover it with fake smiles and hope no one sees past our facade.

We're told by pastors and church leaders that all wounds heal over time and that we need to forgive the one who hurt or offended us. "Forgiveness is the key to our joy and peace," and "If we just surrender our pain to Christ, we will find the ability to forgive our offender."

Counselors and pastors everywhere talk about the responsibility on the victim's part to offer forgiveness, even if the abuser doesn't ask for it. They say it's our job to forgive and love our enemy. "Give it to Christ," they preach. "Forgive and go in peace. Our unforgiveness is a poison, so why hang on to it? Just forgive and be free."

It all sounds so simple and spiritual, so why doesn't it seem to work? If the Pastor said it, then it should work. And if it's not working, I must be doing something wrong.

And why does all the responsibility fall on me, the victim? Doesn't anyone realize I'm the one who is hurting? Doesn't anyone understand the damage that my abuser caused? I didn't ask for this. They took advantage of me and my trust and smashed it into the dirt. They stole my joy, ripped it into a million pieces, and left me broken, so why do I have to do all the work by forgiving them to find my peace? That kind of damage and pain doesn't just go away by simply saying, "I Forgive You."

Every time I see my offenders or hear their names mentioned, the emotional pain comes rushing back, and I feel sick in the pit of my stomach. I take extraordinary measures to avoid being in the same room as that person. What I feel inside after seeing them is so un-Christlike and uncomfortable.

Why do they get to go free after what they did to me, and I'm the one who has to suffer like this? Isn't it only fair that they feel the same amount of pain?

If I'm indeed a child of God, I shouldn't be having these types of thoughts or feelings against another person. Doesn't the Bible say I'm supposed to love my enemy? Me? Love them? How? I don't even LIKE them; how am I supposed to LOVE them? Am I even a Christian? God? Where are you? Why am I having all these thoughts, and why does it still hurt? Why can't I forgive and forget, as the Pastor said? What's wrong with me?

Do these questions sound familiar? Maybe someone you know and love has asked these same questions. Perhaps you have asked them for yourself and don't know where to look to find the answers. If so, then this book is for you.

YOU'RE NOT ALONE!

I may not be a psychologist, but I'm no stranger to God's Word. I'm also no stranger to these genuine and raw emotions that never seem to disappear. These feelings and thoughts have run through my heart and mind thousands of times, haunting me for years.

It's funny how we can find a small measure of comfort in knowing we're not alone in our pain and suffering. It's incredible to me just how many people have experienced abuse in their lives. The abuse or offense comes in many forms, some worse than others, but the pain and scars left behind are very similar. The inability to forgive is a widespread struggle for many victims of abuse.

So why do so many people struggle with forgiveness? Because many people don't understand what forgiveness is. We have this concept that forgiveness is an act on our part that we can turn on or off. All we have to do is forget about our pain and forgive our offender, and then we can go forward in freedom and victory.

Well, it sounds nice, but it doesn't work that easily. It's not that simple. There's so much to this area of forgiveness that is misunderstood and not appropriately taught in churches. Because we misunderstand it, we have unrealistic expectations about forgiveness. When things don't turn out as expected, we examine ourselves, wondering where we went wrong and doubting our relationship with Christ.

Satan rejoices in our doubts, and we become so tired from fighting back with minimal results that we ultimately give up the fight. As we grow weary, bitterness and hatred grow in the ripened soil of despair, and we end up suffering a more extraordinary fate than the original offense: defeat and hopelessness.

We become enslaved to our pain like heavy chains that we cannot break free from, while our abusers seem to live in unfair freedom. We keep our struggle hidden from everyone out of shame. God forbid anyone else should discover we're not as strong on the inside as we appear to be.

LOOKING BACK

In the next part, I will dig deep and share from my heart why God called me to write this book. Perhaps you might understand where these emotions were coming from if you knew what I experienced in my life.

There are parts of my story I have kept hidden for years out of fear of what people might think about me once they discover what I have experienced. After attempting to move on from the abuse of my past several times and forget about it, something keeps bringing me back to it like an old ugly scar that won't go away. I try to hide my imperfections, but I know they're there. I can still feel them, and when no one else is around, I remember my abuse and hurt all over again.

Through experience, study, prayer, and counseling, I have discovered some truths about forgiveness that helped me find my place of peace and healing. I have also discovered that my experience of finding recovery might benefit others who are still fighting the same fight that I fought and continue to fight.

Yes, I said it. I continue to fight. While I can finally forgive my abusers, I still suffer from memories and several consequences of my abuse. It doesn't heal overnight.

Forgiveness is an ongoing process of healing that takes time. It's a journey of addressing and letting go of the pain of your abuse and forgiving your abuser. It's not a fun or simple journey, but it must begin if you want to move forward and stop living your life as a victim of your past.

Sharing my story, helping others discover the same truths, and finding healing is the inspiration for this entire book. For years, I've known I would write it someday after my abusers had passed away.

That day has come. I'm sitting here, alone with my laptop, in the house of my abusers, surrounded by the ghosts of my past. It's all coming back to me, fresh and raw. Most of my story is from the haunting memories I shall always have. My sister and father filled in other parts over the years, answering questions I presented to them while searching for explanations.

I put the missing pieces they provided to me together with everything I remembered and finally have a complete story. It isn't a pretty story, but it's mine.

Scott Green

PART I

MY STORY

1

———

IN THE BEGINNING

My parents met and fell in love in Charlotte, North Carolina, and were married in September 1962. My sister was born one year later, and they were a happy family.

For six years, Dad worked for a radio station, and Mom rode horses and dreamed of one day moving beyond being a full-time, stay-at-home parent. She was eager to re-enter the workforce, but in late 1968, something unexpected happened that changed all her plans; Mom became pregnant with me.

She did not welcome this pregnancy with joy as she did my sister. Having and raising another child would prolong her dreams and life goals. No, I was not a joyful surprise. According to her, having me was a terrible mistake.

Somewhere between my sister and I, another pregnancy miscarried when mom fell off her horse. It wasn't easy; neither she nor Dad ever talked about it for years. But when she became pregnant with me, it overwhelmed Dad with joy and restored his hope after such a significant loss. It was like fate was giving them a second chance. He already had his daughter and now dreamed of having a son. Dad celebrated while Mom began her descent into depression.

Naturally, the doctors warned my mother against riding her horse while pregnant with me, but that didn't stop her. Even after losing one child, she risked it all and rode again. Like before, she fell again from the same horse, whether by accident or on purpose. But by an unexpected twist of fate from above, I survived.

Dad ended up selling Mom's horse to prevent another "accident," and she became very depressed.

IF IT'S A GIRL...

One of Dad's faithful listeners on the radio was an eccentric and wealthy older woman who became very fond of my father and mother. After they met, they became fast friends.

Later, during a dinner date, she asked Mom all kinds of questions about her pregnancy and the day they expected me to arrive. Mom already had one C-section delivery and was planning to have a second one with me. My scheduled date of arrival was June 21, 1969.

After dinner, this woman shared with my parents about her twin sister's untimely death the previous year on June 19. She believed that if my mother gave birth to me on the same day, and if I were a girl, I would be the reincarnation of her late twin sister. If that happened, she vowed to care financially for me and my future and promised I would never want anything. She promised to pay all my medical bills, college tuition, wedding and future expenses. It was an offer my parents could not ignore.

Mom called the doctor's office the next day and rescheduled her delivery date for June 19. Even though Dad still had his heart set on a son, Mom hoped for another girl and the promise of wealth that came with it.

When the day came, and they finally delivered me, Mom raised her head from the surgery table and eagerly asked the doctor, "What is it?" He smiled at her over the sheet and said, "It's a healthy boy!" Without hesitation, she blurted out, "Well, shit!" and fell asleep.

MOM'S ADDICTION

My mother fell deeper into her depression after I was born. Everything she had hoped and dreamed for was gone. She became hooked on antidepressants and other narcotics she got from a shady neighbor who sold them from next door.

She left me alone several times with my sister, who was only six, for extended lengths of time to visit the neighbor while Dad was at work.

My father brought me to the pediatrician with a severe diaper rash twice. After the second incident, he told my father that my rash resulted from pure negligence on my mother's part. He warned my father if he ever saw me in his office like this again, he would call the police and have me taken away and handed over to child protection services. My father swore it wouldn't happen again.

Dad went home and angrily confronted Mom about her whereabouts and neglecting the children. She was never one to back down from a confrontation but to stand up to it and fight back. This fight was the beginning of their marital downfall.

The next day while Dad was at work, my sister witnessed my mother holding me upside down by my feet under the shower in a near-drowning experience while trying to clean my bottom. She was trying to prevent another rash and another confrontation with Dad.

This experience might explain the fear of water I developed. Even as a toddler, I was terrified of the water touching me. To this day, I still have great hesitation before engaging in water sports or beach activities. I endure them for the family's sake, but I am no fan of swimming or large bodies of water unless I am on land, admiring them from a safe distance.

THE SEPARATION

For the next few years, Mom's addiction to narcotics worsened, and so did her marriage. Mom and Dad accused each other of being unfaithful, and my mother fell deeper into her depression.

When I was five years old, she finally reached a breaking point. She packed up the car and brought my sister and me to south Louisiana, where her parents lived, and that's where we stayed until she could put the pieces of her life back together.

My sister and I couldn't understand why we moved away and left Dad behind. Mom said that Dad didn't love us anymore, so we had to move to Louisiana and live with our grandparents. Our hearts were crushed, and Mom made no effort to console us.

Thankfully, my grandparents, whom we called Memaw and Pawpaw, were wonderful God-fearing Christians. They showed lots of love and patience towards us during this difficult time.

After we moved in, Memaw and Pawpaw immediately

noticed Mom's depression and discovered she was taking illegal narcotics. They offered to take care of my sister and me if Mom admitted herself to a local rehabilitation and got herself clean and healthy. Mom realized she was running out of options and that this was her only hope. She finally accepted their offer, said goodbye to us, and checked herself in.

LIFE WITH MEMAW

I have nothing but beautiful memories of my grandparents and their unconditional love for us. Memaw taught Bible stories and prayed with us every night while Mom was away. Living with Memaw was my first experience of a healthy family environment without the heaviness of depression and neglect.

Memaw was a fun-loving soul who loved to spend time with us, always making us smile and laugh. She would cook the most amazing meals, introducing us to new dishes and flavors every night, but her specialty was her desserts. Her homemade chocolate pie had a rich flavor, and I always bargained for extra chores for a second slice. Memaw and Pawpaw provided a loving home for us, and we always felt safe.

Even though my grandparents did all they could for us, my sister and I still greatly missed my father. One night he called to check on us, and my sister confronted him and asked him why he didn't love us anymore. He became shocked and crushed that we would believe such a lie. He sincerely expressed his love to both of us and promised to come and see us soon.

Mom finally completed her time in rehab and moved

back home with us. She and Dad talked on the phone, agreed to give their marriage a second chance, and planned for us to become a family again.

Dad sold our home up north and moved south to reunite with us. He bought a new home, and we became a family again. Life was starting to look brighter.

2

ROUND TWO

Dad took on a new job selling cars and worked his way to becoming a salesperson and trainer for the National Motor Club. He started traveling nationwide for weeks, selling memberships and training new salespeople. My sister was old enough to babysit, so Mom decided it was finally time to re-enter the workforce.

She began a new law enforcement career as a radio dispatcher for the Louisiana State Police. Through her hard work and dedication to her job, she quickly advanced her way to the Sheriff's Department in the jail room and finally patrolled the streets.

She was breaking new ground as one of the first women to enter a career that was initially thought of as a "Man's World." She fought long and hard to be accepted and respected by her male peers. Her identity changed. Her personality changed. Everything changed.

Dad was traveling most of the time, and Mom started working the night shift, leaving us at home alone. She would arrive home early in the morning and sleep all day while we were in school. She was always tired, and the pressure and stress she faced at her job were more than she could handle.

It didn't take long before she sought the comforts of narcotics again to help her cope with the changes in her new career, and that's when the abuse started at home.

It only happened when Dad was away. She never took her aggression out on me when he was home; she knew he loved me dearly and would do anything to protect me from her attacks. So she waited until he went away for another week or two, and that's when the abuse took place.

One morning when I was in third grade, she came home exhausted from work and woke my sister and me up for school. I usually had about 30 - 45 minutes to eat breakfast and get ready before the bus entered our neighborhood. Breakfast was always cereal or toast, and we fixed it ourselves.

She came down the hall and stopped at my door. "Why isn't your room clean?" she barked from the doorway.

"We were watching TV last night. I was going to clean it today." I answered in fear.

"You're damn right you will. You better not step one foot outside this room until it is spotless and you're ready for school. And if you miss the bus, I'm not driving you. I will beat your ass, and you will walk to school. Do you under-stand me?"

"Yes, ma'am." Then she went into her bedroom to get into her nightclothes and sleep till late afternoon.

I worked fast to clean my room and prepare for school on time. Once I had done everything Mom expected, I stepped out of my room with a drinking glass I had left overnight on my nightstand. I brought it into the kitchen, and somehow, while attempting to place it in the sink, I dropped it. The glass landed on its edge and shattered all over the kitchen floor with a loud crash. I held my breath and froze.

"What the Hell?" I could hear Mom storming down the hall in a rage as I frantically started picking up the large pieces of glass.

"WHAT HAPPENED?" she screamed as she rounded the corner into the kitchen.

"I'm sorry, it just slipped," I said as I picked up the large shards. When Mom saw the mess I had made, she screamed, reached out, grabbed me around the throat with a forceful grip, and started choking me while backing me up against the wall. I grabbed at her hands and gasped for air.

I tried to escape her grip but lost balance and fell backward, and landed on the ground next to the broken glass. Before I knew it, she was screaming and spitting, climbing on top of me, and pinning me down under her knees so I couldn't escape. Then, with clenched fists, she started swinging as hard as she could on my head, my face, my chest, and anywhere her fists would land as I screamed out and cried, begging her to stop.

My sister heard all the screaming between us and came racing into the kitchen. Once she saw what was happening, she immediately jumped in, grabbed my mother's arms from behind in mid-swing, and held them in the air while yelling for me to get up and run. I struggled to climb out from under my screaming mother while my sister restrained her.

Once I got to my feet, I grabbed my books and ran as fast as I could past my mother and sister and out the door to catch the bus, crying all the way. I was terrified to come home that afternoon, but I was even more terrified to tell anyone what happened.

· · ·

WHY JUST ME?

The abuse and beatings became a regular occurrence whenever Dad was away. If she wasn't beating me, she told me I was a mistake and that she never wanted me. I was Satan's child and God's curse on her life. Several times, she said how she wished I had never been born.

When a child hears these things regularly, it doesn't take long before he believes them. I would sit in my room at night after a beating and look out the window, weeping and sobbing and praying for my father to come home. That was the only time I felt safe from her wrath. I told no one what my mother did to me out of fear that it would only bring another round of beatings.

Between the beatings, I couldn't help but wonder why Mom never treated my sister the way she treated me. She was much kinder to her, more patient, and she seemed to like her more than me. Why was I the only one she treated this way? Was I that horrible as a child?

As far as I can remember, I was just as normal as the next kid. I had my share of mischief but was afraid to challenge or rebel against her rules and demands. If I ever stood up or spoke back to her, I knew what would happen to me, so I didn't. I did everything I could not to anger or upset her.

Mom never allowed me to have friends inside the house, but my friends would come over when she was away. We would play outside under the carport together. One day, she came home and found about ten kids playing under the carport. She started screaming and shouting for them to leave and threw rocks from the rock garden until they did. My friends learned to stay away, and I became very lonely.

I dreaded the most when she came home from the night shift during the summer. She was tired and needed the house to be entirely silent for sleep. One thing that relaxed her was when someone took a toothpick and dragged it slowly across her arms, legs, feet, or face.

She would get dressed for bed, lay down, and force me to sit quietly in the room next to her in the dark and drag a toothpick over her face or limbs until she fell asleep. After a while, my arm would grow tired, and I would stop, hoping she was already sleeping, but then she would speak out, "Keep going; I'm not asleep yet."

If I expressed I was tired or wanted a break, she would call me selfish and force me to keep going. Every morning, I would sit there in the dark, dragging that toothpick over her with tears running down my face, hoping she would fall fast asleep and never wake up.

One morning after she fell asleep, I sneaked out and played quietly in my room. I accidentally bumped into a bookshelf and made a loud noise. I froze and waited to see if it woke her up. After a moment, I heard her yell out my name. She came into the hallway and asked what had happened. I apologized and told her what I did and that I was sorry. She stood there, and I waited in fear for her response.

She raised her hand and slapped me hard across my face. "Next time, you'll be more careful before you decide to wake anyone up when they're trying to sleep." Then she walked past me and into the bathroom. I stood there with my hand covering my burning cheek and cried quietly to myself.

THE BREAKDOWN

Since my home life was becoming increasingly intense,

my grades began to suffer in school. I was in fifth grade, and focusing on my assignments was difficult. I had a teacher who acted like she enjoyed handing out poor grades and didn't care about offering much help for improvement. She handed me my report card to bring home to have my parents sign and bring back to class.

The teachers would staple our report cards to keep us from seeing and changing our grades. However, I could still peel back a corner just enough to see an F in math and another in spelling. Dad was coming home that night, so maybe I could delay showing it until he got home and avoid Mom's wrath.

When I arrived home, Mom was already awake and waiting for me at the door. "Where's your report card?" My heart sank, and I looked at the floor. "Give it to me now."

I slowly reached into my backpack and pulled it out. Mom reached down and snatched it from my hands, and then I waited in panic for what came next.

She ripped it open and looked inside. After a moment, she said, "Well, your father's coming home, and he will not like this one bit." I said nothing.

"You think your father enjoys coming home to find out his son is a dumbass?"

"No, ma'am."

"What the hell have you been doing in school? Playing with yourself?" I still didn't answer her. She took the report card and swung back to strike me, and I immediately ducked out of reach and started crying.

"Why are you crying? I didn't hit you." I didn't know how to respond anymore except with more tears. Oh, how I wanted Dad to come home so bad right then. I knew my grades would disappoint him, but at least he wouldn't hit me for them.

"SHUT UP AND STOP CRYING," she demanded.

I tried, but I just couldn't. "Fine, keep crying. You're just doing that so your father can come in and see his little drama queen and then jump on me again. You LOVE to see us fight, don't you?"

"No, ma'am." I wiped my face, but the tears wouldn't stop.

"You know you're the reason we're always fighting, don't you? If you weren't here, I'd have a happier marriage." Her words stung almost as bad as her fists. "You better shut up before I give you something to cry about."

As I look back on that day, I recognize now I had an emotional breakdown.

I honestly believed everything she said about me. When she said I was the source and cause of all her grief, I believed it. She said I was for so many years, so I carried the guilt of everything that went wrong because somehow I thought it was my fault.

But then Dad would finally come home, and I got to experience a break from her abuse for a few days.

WHEN DAD CAME HOME

I loved when Dad was home because he and I would do things together. One of my favorite things was going to the movies. Every weekend, whenever he was home, we would pack up the car with pillows and blankets, and the whole family would go to the drive-in and watch double features.

I enjoyed these moments because it was the closest we got to being an average family. My sister and I would hide under a blanket on the backseat's floor, so Dad would only have to pay for him and Mom. In between the movies, Dad always took me to the concession stand. He bought me my favorite orange drink in a round plastic orange container. I would stick my straw and drink it as fast as possible. Sometimes, he bought me two of them.

If we weren't going to the drive-in, he would take me with him on Saturday afternoons to the cinema, where we saw all kinds of entertaining films together. Comedy, drama, action, musicals, and even horror. My dad introduced me to all the best.

Once when I was nine years old, he took me to see Jon Voight, Faye Dunaway, and Ricky Schroder in *The Champ*. I didn't know what this movie was about, but it didn't matter. I was with my dad, and I felt safe.

This movie was a heartbreaking story about the love between a father and a son. There were so many moments in the film that made us both cry, especially the ending. Not only was it the saddest movie I ever saw, but it was also the first time I ever saw my dad cry. It made me realize it was okay to express that emotion. Instead of screaming at me for crying, he handed me a handkerchief, and we cried together. It was almost a bond we shared. That moment will last forever in my heart.

Later that day, we ate fast food and had a wonderful time together. I didn't want the day to end because I knew it was almost time for him to leave again. After a few moments, I broke down and told him what Mom had done to me while he was away.

He became very silent, and after a moment, he hung his head. "I'm very sorry, Scott. I'll talk to your mother." That's all he said. Did he believe me? Would he talk to her? Would she stop beating me, or would she become even angrier and blame me for causing more trouble between them?

I was more afraid this time. Dad was still leaving, and I would be alone with Mom again, and there was nothing he could do to stop her. I felt hopeless and afraid.

3

____

HOME ALONE

Mom wasn't my only abuser. While it's true that my sister would sometimes come to my rescue and help me escape or avoid Mom during her wrath, there were many times when Mom was at work and left me to my sister's torture. I was only ten, and she was 16, and we certainly had our share of sibling rivalry.

I remember the regular fights that we had. My sister would cram me into the toy box and sit on top of it, locking me inside while I beat on the lid, screamed, and cried for long periods to be released.

She once begged to put me in a dress with makeup. I said "NO," but she promised to do all the chores if I let her do this one thing, so I finally gave up resisting. After she dressed and made me up, she tossed me outside the front door in front of my friends. She locked the door behind me, leaving me humiliated, experiencing my friends' haunting laughter. I had to run around the back of the house and come in through the back door, finding my sister in the corner laughing hysterically at me.

Of course, sometimes, I would get revenge, like tossing a glass of ice water at her while she was sleeping. I regretted that action after she picked me up and threw me hard across the bed, causing my foot to crash through the bedroom window. This time, Dad was the one who got angry, and Mom thought it was funny.

Then there's the time when she played golf while I was standing too close behind her. She wasn't looking and swung the metal club backward. That club landed right in my face under my left eye, creating a bloody gash that ended with me going to the emergency room and getting 13 stitches. These sibling rivalry stories are the traditional tales that brothers and sisters laugh about and entertain the family with at Thanksgiving and get-togethers.

But then there were other times. Dad was away, and Mom was at work, leaving me alone with my sister. She had invented a new "Let's Pretend" game based on some adult romance novels she found in my mother's room.

I was much too young to understand the reality of what was happening, but that game of "Let's Pretend" led to several months of her sexually experimenting, molesting, and raping me. She told me she was preparing me for when I got older and started dating. She made me believe she was helping me and teaching me how to treat a girl. She didn't want her brother to be inexperienced.

The sexual abuse continued until I was finally old enough to realize that what she was doing to me was wrong. I became disgusted and ashamed and eventually refused to play her games. I carried a heavy burden and disgust from that experience that remains to this very day. The memories of her actions have haunted me for years and have caused me to become very confused about sexuality.

There was a brief time in my life when I questioned my own sexual identity since my experience with women was nothing but abusive, dysfunctional, and degrading. I didn't tell anyone what I was struggling with out of shame. I carried that pain with me for years, adding to the trauma of my mother's abuse.

THE PILE OF PORN

One night when Dad was away on another one of his trips, Mom found a collection of girlie magazines in the back of Dad's closet. Instead of complaining and throwing them away, as a typical wife might do, she sat on the floor, leaning against her bed with my sister at her side. They went through each of them, commenting on the naked pictures and laughing together at the adult cartoons.

I walked in on them, wondering what was so funny, and saw them gleefully peering through the pile of pornography. My face flushed with embarrassment, and I turned quickly to leave, but Mom told me to sit next to my sister, grab a magazine, and start flipping through it.

She made me search for and show them any cartoons I came across so she and my sister could laugh together. I felt so ashamed, awkward, and confused by her instructions. Even at a young age, I knew this was highly inappropriate. Still, I didn't dare disobey and risk another round of her rage.

I nervously flipped through the pages and past the pornographic photos. My mother made me stop several times, drawing attention to the naked women on the pages.

"Look at all these whores and sluts, exposing themselves like that for men to lust over." I kept silent because I didn't know how to respond. "Does this turn you on? Do you like to see women like this?"

"N-no, ma'am," I stuttered.

"They're all whores, and the men who buy this trash are nothing but pigs. These are your father's magazines, and he's a pig for looking at them. These kinds of people are going straight to Hell."

She then made me look at pictures of men doing terrible and nasty things to the women while she and my sister laughed and gawked. I never felt so embarrassed or ashamed. Sitting there like I was in the middle of a horror movie, I knew this was all wrong.

This behavior was a perverted and dysfunctional side of my mother I had never seen before. It not only scared me, but it left me dazed and confused. She finally closed the magazines, put the box back in my dad's closet, and sent me to my room.

I wanted to get up, run away, hide, and never face my mother or sister again. I didn't understand all the different emotions I was feeling. Still, it was a horrifying experience that left me feeling damaged and broken. That night, I sat in my room, crying.

I took one of my father's razor blades and held it against my wrist and thought about all the different ways I could slice my wrist and end it all. I wanted to write a letter and blame my mother and sister so they would know what it was like to carry all the blame and guilt I was hauling around.

No one at school would miss me since I was bullied and laughed at on the bus. No one would miss me at all except my father. The only reason I didn't follow through with killing myself that night was knowing how it might affect him. Instead, I just laid back and cried myself to sleep.

4

FINDING MYSELF

As I got older, the physical beatings ended, but the mental and emotional abuse continued. Mom and Dad continued to have marital problems, and I was always the cause.

Mom lost her job at the Sheriff's Department after accusations surfaced of her having inappropriate relations with co-workers and prisoners. Of course, she vehemently denied all allegations against her.

Years later, my sister confirmed to me the accuracy of those accusations. Mom would use my sister as a decoy by telling Dad she and my sister were going out, and then the two of them would drive to a meeting point where one of her male friends was waiting for her. She would leave my sister in her car alone and go off in the other vehicle with the man for a brief time.

My sister told me how hard this was on her and how difficult it was to keep this a secret from Dad. She loved her mom but lost a lot of respect for her after that experience.

At some point, when my sister was 19, she blindsided

Mom by coming out that she was a homosexual and in love with another woman. For the first time, Mom turned her wrath toward my sister.

She never assaulted her physically, but she berated her verbally and emotionally and ended up throwing her out of the house. Dad was heartbroken, but he didn't fight Mom's decision. My sister ended up getting an apartment and exploring her newfound independence.

WHO AM I?

It was 1983. Dad quit his traveling job, and Mom became a full-time secretary for a swimming pool company. Summer was over, and I was in a mess. I was 14, just starting high school, and still trying to find myself. My body was changing, and I was experiencing very confusing emotions and feelings. I was carrying a lot of emotional baggage that weighed heavily on me over the years.

I figured I should try some sports, so I entered track and field and the wrestling team at school, but I failed to measure up to everyone around me. That sure didn't help my self-esteem, and it didn't take long to realize I was not athletic.

I remembered playing drums in the band for a year, but that didn't satisfy me either, so I got involved in drama and the choir. That's when I discovered my joy in singing and the performing arts. Not only did I enjoy it, but I also wasn't half bad. I earned a top spot in the honor and all-state choir and participated in the school musicals. I finally found my place.

I soon discovered that drama and choir students are certainly not that popular. Still, I found others like myself, who were also from broken and dysfunctional families. We became a tight little group of rejected misfits who met weekly with the school guidance counselor, sharing our stories and burdens. We became our own little support system for one another, and that's how I met my new friend Carla.

I'M NOT ALONE

One morning on the school bus, I noticed that Carla had thick wristbands. After I questioned her, she confided that she tried to cut her wrists because her father was sexually abusing her. She tried to tell her mom, but her mom wouldn't believe her.

We talked for a while, and I encouraged Carla to speak with our school counselor, whom we both loved and trusted. Carla agreed, and I walked with her to the office for support.

The school called Carla's mother into a private meeting that afternoon, and the counselor informed her of her daughter's confession. Her mom was now facing the possibility that the accusation against her husband was true. She went home and finally confronted her husband, which ended in a huge fight.

Regardless of the turnout, I was proud of Carla for her bravery in taking her stand and letting someone know.

The following day, Carla's father got up early, and as Carla left for school, he told her goodbye. She climbed on the school bus, sat next to me, and we drove away. As soon as we were out of sight, he told his wife to stay inside the house, and then he took his rifle and went into the backyard and shot himself.

When I heard what happened, I became overwhelmed with grief and guilt. I knew that if Carla didn't tell someone, she might have died, but I didn't count on how he might respond or how she would carry the weight of guilt for exposing his dirty secrets. Our friendship became strained after that, and I felt responsible.

I thought about my abuse at home and what might happen if I shared everything I was going through. My sister already told me if I told anyone what she did to me, she would kill herself. I vowed I would never tell. I was too ashamed and afraid, so I kept her secret out of fear of what she might do.

THE WRONG CROWD

It was the summer of '84, and I turned 15. I experimented with many new things, trying to find a place where I felt accepted and belonged. On weekends, I got involved with a group of new friends who were older and invited me to new places, nightclubs, bars, parties, and *The Rocky Horror Picture Show*. They introduced me to a new culture, and I met people who expressed themselves as Punk, Goth, Metalhead, and New Wave. It was the only crowd where I didn't find rejection at every turn.

Suddenly, I found myself surrounded by pot, alcohol, and drugs. Still, I never became interested in experimenting with any of those things. I watched their frightening but entertaining effects on everyone around me, but I chose just to say no.

I experimented with other things. Several people much older than me sexually took advantage of me, and to be accepted, I allowed them. It didn't take long to realize I was being used for their temporary lusts and gratification. They had no intention of keeping me around. They disappeared as quickly as they came, leaving me even more miserable, lonely, and rejected.

When school started again, I remembered attempting to reinvent myself and identify with the New Wave and Punk culture. I wore chains, long trench coats with bulky sleeves rolled up, high-top shoes, pierced one ear, and tried my best to look like a Duran Duran music group member.

I dated girls with shaved designs and blue streaks in their hair and smoked pot. Still, each of those relationships ended in the most typical teenage dramatic breakup straight out of a John Hughes '80s movie.

Even among my new colorful friends, I struggled to find myself. My grades continued to drop, right along with my self-esteem. No matter how hard I tried, I couldn't find anything to make me feel accepted and fulfilled. I toned down my appearance and spent the rest of the school year lying low and depressed.

5

____

THE TURNAROUND

At the beginning of a hot summer in '85, Dad came home with a startling announcement: We were going to attend church. This announcement was a real shock because we had never been to church together as a family. I had gone a few years before with a neighborhood friend, but we were not churchgoing people as a family.

Mom grew up in a substantial Christian home but abandoned her faith after moving away alone. She had the knowledge and some understanding of biblical things, but she applied none of it to her life. She certainly was no Christian. But once we started going to church together, she quickly tapped into her religious knowledge. She became an instant expert on all things biblically and Christian-related.

The local church we visited welcomed us immediately and made us feel at home. It was small and traditional, but the Pastor did a fantastic job preaching the need for salvation.

One Sunday, they announced a four-week movie series

coming soon on Saturday nights based on the book of Revelation, titled *A Thief in the Night.* Since our family loved movies, Dad committed to taking us to see them.

They filmed the movies in the early and mid-'70s and had a meager budget with amateur acting. The film critic in me came out instantly, noticing every fault and blooper. I wondered if I could last all four weeks of this series, but as the exciting and suspenseful story unfolded, it eventually drew me in and held my attention.

By the end of the second week, I went home with a heaviness in my heart. I decided to go for a walk by myself around the block.

For the first time, I had an honest talk with God. The sky was clear, the air was cool, and I could feel His presence with me. I repented everything I knew and invited Jesus to come and live inside my heart, just like the Pastor instructed every week at church. By the end of my walk, it felt like a heavy load had lifted from me, and I suddenly didn't feel as lonely as before.

We not only finished that film series but became members of that church. Mom made some effort to be kinder at home, and Dad finally gave his life to Christ, just as I did. Our home life was indeed getting better.

Mom no longer called me the Demonic Spawn of Satan since my sister became a lesbian. My sister was embracing her new alternate lifestyle and friends and drifting further and further from the family.

I was getting older, and Mom and I still had our difficult moments, but they were becoming fewer and further apart. We all gave this new life as a Christian family a real chance.

I got to go on a summer youth trip away from home for

an entire week. It was a refreshing and welcoming change of pace and surroundings for me. Once I arrived there, I opened my suitcase to unpack my things and found a note tucked under my shirt. It was from my mother. I unfolded it, and it read:

Thank you for taking us with you. We love you, and I didn't want you to get lonesome without us. Have a great time, but don't put the good times before God. This is a great opportunity for others to see how God works in your life. Hurry home to us.

OXOXOXOX
Mamma

That might be one of the most loving things Mom has ever done for me. I thought about how Mom changed her ways towards me since my sister came out and we started attending church together. Perhaps now, things would be different. Maybe this is what we needed all along to bring us closer together. Oh, how I loved what God was doing for our family.

A FRESH START

Because I was the new teenager at church who loved my new faith in Christ, I didn't fit in well with the other teenagers. I felt like an outsider or an intruder whenever I attended one of their youth meetings. Privately, they accused me of loving Jesus too much and claimed no one wanted to be around me.

The last place I expected to experience rejection was at church. I thought these kids would be different from the ones at school, but I quickly learned that being in church doesn't automatically make you a Christian.

Since Christ was changing my life and I was doing well in the choir at school, the Pastor invited me to lead the song service in the church. It opened up some new experiences and training for me, but it also added to my rejection from the other teenagers. I felt like a misfit, just like I did at school, and I was becoming lonelier. The adults loved and welcomed me, but I was still rejected among my peers.

In that small church, I learned how to act, talk, and present myself to others as a strong Christian; on the surface, I did that very well. But I still secretly struggled with some things inside, like confusion, loneliness, insecurity, and trying to find a place where I fit in and didn't feel like an outcast.

As much as I enjoyed my new identity in Christ, I felt like there was something else I was lacking. I knew I was on the right path to finding the needed answers, but I hadn't found them yet.

When school started back up, I was eager to share my new faith with my old friends whom I hadn't seen since last semester. I arrived at school and met everyone in our traditional meeting spot on campus.

We all welcomed each other back and started sharing about our summer activities. I didn't hold back. I shared how I started attending church and became a Christian and how different it made me feel. My friends immediately labeled me a Jesus Freak and quickly dismissed me.

I didn't expect another round of rejection. I thought my friends would be happy for me and want to know more about it. Wow, I thought, even my closest friends didn't want to be around me. I never felt lonelier in all my life. Being a Christian was already cramping my social life at church, and now it was also causing trouble for me at school. At least Jesus had twelve friends; I had none.

TODD AND CHANCE

God must have heard my prayers because that's when I met Todd and Chance, the new guys in school. They were two typical teenage boys who were best friends and loved martial arts, girls, and comic books, but something about them set them apart from everyone else. These two guys passionately loved Jesus. I mean, they were ON FIRE for Christ. I have met no one quite like them.

Todd was the brave one. Everyone called him "The Preacher Kid," and he would preach to anyone who would listen and even those who wouldn't. Chance was his faithful sidekick, always nearby and consistently praying and cheering him on.

Todd would stand up during lunch and preach to all the surrounding students with no shame or fear. He didn't seem to care about being rejected. Some football players would mock him, and everyone would laugh, but that didn't stop him. He kept preaching. One or two of the larger boys would threaten to beat him and rip him into little pieces if he didn't shut up. He responded, "Yes, you could, but every little piece would still love you, and so will Jesus!"

I sat there, amazed at his boldness, and wished I could be just like that. Why should I care what people think of me? Why should I allow rejection to steal my joy? These guys experienced rejection, just like I did, but they still had fun. They counted it all joy. I read that in the Bible, too.

> *Consider it pure joy, my brothers and sisters, whenever you face trials of many kinds because you know that the testing of your faith produces perseverance. (James 1:2-3)*

I was tired of feeling rejected and mistreated everywhere I went. These two guys didn't care about rejection; they were more passionate about their relationship with Christ. I wanted what they had.

We immediately became fast friends, and the three of us became a trio, like the Three Musketeers. They invited me over after school each day and to spend the night on weekends. We shared our testimonies, studied the Bible together, prayed, and laughed till the early hours of the morning. I finally found some real friends who I was proud to call my brothers. It wasn't long before I visited their youth service at Community Chapel.

When I arrived for the first time, I remember walking into that youth room and seeing something I had never seen before. I saw about 200 young people my age standing on their feet, with their hands lifted in the air and singing. Not just singing a song out of a hymn book, but genuinely worshiping from the heart.

"I love you, Lord," they sang. "And I lift my voice, to worship you, oh my soul rejoice."

When I heard that sound, I experienced a stirring in my heart I had never experienced before. Tears ran down my face, and my heart swelled. Whatever this was, this is what I was hungry for. This experience is what I needed.

For the first time, it all became real to me. It was the presence of an almighty God responding to his children, who were passionately and eagerly seeking more of Him. I wanted nothing more, nothing else, just THIS. I discovered that night the presence of God was more pleasing, more satisfying, and more fulfilling than anything else I had ever experienced. He was here, and His spirit filled my heart with His love for me. I never wanted to leave or for that moment to end.

Then the Youth Pastor preached a stirring message about God's endless love for us, and I hung on every word as if he were talking directly to me. It was like he could see inside my heart and knew what I needed to hear.

When he finished, they opened the altars and invited anyone who wanted more of Jesus to come forward. I learned that while I wanted more of Jesus, Jesus wanted more of me. He chose me and sent His Spirit to draw me into His presence. I fell to my knees, wept, and surrendered everything to Him.

That night changed my life. My walk with God just entered a whole new level. I couldn't wait until the following week to experience it again. When I got home, I turned on some worship music in my bedroom and discovered I didn't have to wait till next week. God was showing up in my bedroom, and I was experiencing His presence all over again.

So this is what Memaw meant when she talked about having a personal relationship with Jesus. For the first time, it became personal to me. It wasn't about being accepted by people or winning their approval; it was all about His acceptance of me and me receiving Him in return. This is the difference between religion and a relationship.

My life continued to change as I became a student of the

Bible. His words came alive in my heart. My attitude changed, my life changed, and everything changed. I felt free and alive, finally finding a place where I belonged and a church where people accepted me for who I was.

And then, just like that, it started again.

6

SHE'S BACK!

Mom's newfound love and kindness at home quickly faded into hurtful and cutting remarks about the new church I was attending. She accused the church and my new friends of being a cult, trying to take me away from the small church where we all went together as a family. She resorted to cursing and screaming about how Satan brainwashed me and that I needed to stop going to that church.

"Mom," I replied calmly, "if you knew what was going on in my brain before I started going to that church, you would agree my brain needed washing." I meant no disrespect, but I had to speak the truth. She would curse and threaten that if I didn't stop going, she would pack her bags, leave home, and go live with her parents, which would be my fault.

I felt like Mom was trying to rip everything I found away from me and hold me hostage in the church, which made me feel lonely and rejected.

Out of respect for God's Word, which clearly stated that the husband was the head of the family and the home priest,

I went to my father. I explained that the new church meant a lot to me and that Mom threatened me if I continued to go. He listened as I told him I would honor his decision, and if he wanted me back at the small church with him and Mom, I would respect that, but my heart was no longer there. I wanted to be where I felt like I belonged.

Once I pleaded my case, I waited. I trusted God enough to accept his conclusive answer, even if it was one I didn't want to hear. I knew honoring Dad's decision was keeping the authority God set up over me.

After a moment, he admitted he had noticed a tremendous change in my life since I started attending Community Chapel. He could see that I was happier and more at peace. He finally agreed, and I had his full support to go to the church of my choice. Mom was not pleased with his decision.

The following Sunday, I went to Community Chapel, stayed with friends through lunch, and returned to church that night. When I returned home, I discovered that Mom had packed her bags and moved out. Memaw was becoming very sick with throat cancer, so Mom used that to justify her move into their home to help care for her in her last days, yet Mom still made it out to be my fault.

During the week, I came home from school, Dad would be at work, and I found brief notes around the house addressed to him. Mom had been over during the day while I was at school.

I read his notes; they expressed her love and how she missed him. When I got to my room, I found another brief note waiting for me to read. Instead of finding another love note, I found hateful, hurtful words accusing me of being selfish, inconsiderate, and coming in between her and Dad, keeping them apart. Once again, I caused her pain and suffering, and she ensured I knew about it.

PIZZA NIGHT

After several months, Memaw passed away, Mom moved back home, and our relationship remained very strained. I did everything I could to keep my distance and the peace. My sister took a job up north and moved away with her girlfriend. We didn't communicate for a good while. Mom was heartbroken after she left, taking out her frustrations on me.

Dad and I tried our best to keep peace at home. Dad would make plans from time to time for us to do something together as a family. One night, the three of us went to our favorite pizza spot and sat inside, waiting to order our favorite meat-lovers pizza. I looked around the restaurant and noticed some friendly people I knew from Community Chapel. I smiled and waved, and they politely smiled and waved back. "Who is that?" Dad asked.

"Just some people from church. I know their son from the youth group."

"You mean that demonic cult church?" Mom quickly quipped. I didn't respond because I didn't want to start anything. The night was going reasonably well, and I didn't want to trigger another argument.

After Dad ordered, the conversation was going fairly decent, but nothing of great substance—just a light casual chat between Dad and me. Mom only took part when we directly addressed her; even then, her responses were short and cold. When the pizza arrived, I passed the plates and counted the slices. Mom raised her head and asked, "Why are you counting the pieces?"

"So we'll know how many slices we each get," I replied.

She paused and then blurted out rather loudly, "There you go again, thinking only of yourself. Have we ever denied you food? Are you afraid someone might eat one of your slices? I can't believe you are so greedy that you must count the slices and tell us how many we can eat. We sure don't want to deny you any food."

I sank back in my chair, afraid to move or do anything, knowing people around us could hear every word, including the family from church. Dad tried to get her attention to stop making a scene, but she got even louder.

"You're always coming to his defense. He can do no wrong around you. Why don't you and your perfect little prince eat the whole damn thing without me. I can't sit here now and eat after this."

She turned to me. "You see what you did? Your selfishness caused another war between your father and me. I hope you're happy. I'll be waiting in the car. Enjoy the damn pizza; I hope you choke on it!" She grabbed her purse and stormed out of the restaurant with almost every eye on her and then us.

"I'm so sorry, Scott," Dad offered. "You did nothing wrong. You know how your mother is."

"Yes," my voice cracked, "I do."

7

A NEW DIRECTION

After I finished high school, I started working as a server in a local steakhouse and dating Suzanne, the most wonderful girl I had ever met. She was as passionate about her walk with God as I was. Her faith and love for Christ are what attracted me to her. We were already great friends for two years, and we finally moved our friendship into a dating relationship.

Mom remained very silent and distant, except for the occasional times she would offer her insulting opinions on my life, my church, and even my relationship with Suzanne. Nothing I ever did could please her. Life at home got more and more difficult.

I finally entered a full-time ministry training bible school at our church. I moved out of my parents' home and lived with a host family from the church for an entire year. It solved the mounting tension growing at home.

Once I moved in with my host family, I witnessed what a real Christian family should resemble. Nightly devotions, prayers for one another, love, and encouragement abounded in that family, and they took me in as one of their own. It was a pleasant and whole-new experience that I embraced and welcomed.

After graduating, I worked as a youth pastor in Mississippi. I proposed marriage to Suzanne, who waited patiently for me. My father couldn't be happier with our plans for marriage and my new job, even though he would miss me terribly.

Mom, however, made it very clear she disapproved of my bride-to-be and would not be attending our wedding celebration. Mom made many accusations against Suzanne and excuses for why she disapproved of her. Still, the real reason was that she was from "THAT DAMN CHURCH."

Mom tried everything to break us up, including making a phone call to Suzanne's sister, Tammy, attempting to draw her into a plot to talk us out of the marriage and to change our plans. Thankfully, Tammy refused to join in, and she celebrated our goals together. Suzanne's sister was not only supportive and loving, but she also became like a new sister to me, and the whole family welcomed me as their own.

Mom finally realized I wasn't budging from my plans. She wasn't getting her way, so she reluctantly accepted our marriage and even agreed to attend the ceremony. However, she would not take part as the groom's mother.

TAKING A STAND

Over the years, Mom and I continued having disagreements, fights, and arguments. She never failed to blame me for everything that went wrong in her life or her marriage.

Suzanne and I left our position as youth pastors in

Mississippi and took another youth pastor's position in Arkansas.

After about six months of being away from home, I invited Dad to come and visit us in Rogers, which was not too far from his hometown of Little Rock. It thrilled him to make the journey and see us for the weekend.

When Mom heard what we were planning, she got on the phone and interrupted. "What do you think you're doing?"

"I'm inviting dad to come to visit us; why?" I said without hesitation; I had done nothing wrong.

"You're father does not need to be driving to Arkansas. How can you be so inconsiderate to ask your father to go all the way up there and leave me here alone?"

"He doesn't have to come alone. You're welcome to come to visit with him. There's plenty of room for both of you. Wouldn't you like to see Little Rock again? You always said you wanted to visit the library and research your family tree."

"I have no intention of ever staying under the same roof with you and Suzanne."

"Well, that's your choice, but dad wants to visit us, and we're open to him coming."

"You are the most selfish person. All you think about is yourself and what you want. You never think about how your wants will affect other people. Your selfishness and inconsiderate ways have always come between your father and me. Our lives would be much better if you just minded your business and quit trying to interfere with our marriage."

"How am I selfish by just inviting him to visit us?"

"You're putting your father at risk of driving that far away from home, and if anything happened to him, I would be left all alone, and it would be all your fault. Now I have to try and talk him out of coming to see you, and he will be upset with me. Thanks a lot for causing another fight between your father and me."

It was at this moment that my patience reached its limit. For the first time in my life, I spoke up. "No. You will NOT turn this around on me and make this my fault. I will NOT accept responsibility for ruining your marriage. If you're having problems, it's your fault. A marriage takes two people, and I don't even live there anymore. I'm tired of taking responsibility for everything that goes wrong in your life and marriage, and I won't do it anymore. The guilt trip stops NOW."

I paused for a moment, waiting for a response. All I heard was the slamming of the phone. Mom hung up on me, and we didn't talk again for about three months.

It was a glorious three months, and I felt like I had accomplished something huge in my life. To this day, I have never regretted my response to her. I only wish I had said it sooner.

I was proud of finally taking my stand with her. Still, deep inside, I dreamed of having a heart-to-heart talk with her and being able to put our past behind us and move forward as adults. If only I could hear her say just once, "I'm sorry," I could easily forgive her, and we could start all over, or at least become friends.

LIKE A CHECKERBOARD

Over the next couple of years, Suzanne and I felt like checker pieces on the checkerboard of life. We left Rogers after a year and took another position as youth pastors closer to home in Pineville, La.

After five challenging years, the birth of my two beautiful daughters, and a fantastic ministry experience, we moved back home. We took a refreshing long break from the ministry where I could focus on being a husband and father to my children.

I returned to my position as a server in a restaurant, worked my way to becoming a trainer, and finally accepted a position as an office manager for an offshore boat company. That gave me managerial experience before God called me back into ministry after being out for nine years.

We finally answered the call of God again and moved back to Mississippi, to the same church we started as Youth Pastors; but this time, they voted us in as the head pastor. God had an exciting and unexpected twist for our lives, bringing us full circle and back to pastor the same church.

After several years, my sister finally ended her relation- ship with her special friend. She moved back home with our mom and dad. She fell into a deep depression, gained weight, and physically let herself go. Even though they had their moments of disagreements, Mom was happy to have her daughter home again. They became closer and bonded more vitally than ever before.

My sister finally gave her life to Christ and started reading and studying her Bible. This change in her life encouraged Mom to become more active again, so they studied the Bible together.

I tried to take advantage of Mom's renewed interest in Bible study and attempted to have theological discussions with her. I was trying to find some common ground, but that didn't work either. She continued to accuse me of being brainwashed and misleading a whole church of innocent people down the path of deception. It became evident that we could not discuss biblical things with each other without her becoming frustrated and unable to change my viewpoints.

The conversation always ended in another round of hurtful words and heavy tension between us. I attempted to avoid Mom altogether.

8

THE FIRST CONFRONTATION

One day, when I was visiting town, I wanted to discuss some things with my sister. The time felt right, and I needed to address our past because it had caused me so much turmoil in my life. I waited for the right moment when I knew I had her undivided attention.

I brought up to her that there were lots of things from my childhood that I remembered. I casually mentioned Mom's abuse and then added how I remembered what she did to me.

There was an awkward silence, and I held my breath, waiting for her response. After another moment, I saw the tears welling up in her eyes. She tried to speak, but no words came out. Instead, she cleared her throat, swallowed hard, and then broke down and cried.

My sister never denied or tried to shift the blame as Mom typically did. Instead of making excuses, she owned up to what she did and wept hard while expressing how sorry she was.

I listened as she shared how much she regretted what

she did to me over the years but was too afraid to bring it up. She hoped I might have forgotten and she would never have to face her sins. She already begged God to forgive her, and now she was begging me to forgive her.

Could Jesus forgive sins like that? Of course, He can and does so when people confess and repent of those sins. The incredible thing about God is His grace and mercy when one of His children repents and says, "Father, forgive me."

But I'm not Jesus. All the years of pain and shame suddenly came rushing back to me. Her abuse has caused several dysfunctions and consequences in my life. Things I still have to pray through and struggle with to this very day. She does not know what she stole from me or how much she caused me to suffer. And just like that, she is asking me to forgive her. Can I?

I never thought it could be possible. I always wondered how people could forgive abuse like this. But when I saw her sitting there, broken and humbled, my heart went to her.

Before I could think it through any longer, I said, "Yes, I forgive you." Then we hugged, we cried, and for the first time in years, I didn't feel disgusted by her touch. I just experienced a miracle—the miracle of an answered prayer and the releasing power of forgiveness flowing through my body.

What made it possible for me to forgive her that day? Other than the strength of Christ, seeing her repent of what she did. It made forgiving her so much easier. She understands and accepts responsibility and humbles herself enough to ask for forgiveness. That wasn't easy for her, and I gained a new respect for her that day.

Yes, I got to experience the miracle of seeing my abuser come to complete repentance. I thought about how very few abuse victims get to witness their abuser asking for forgiveness. This experience doesn't happen very often, and I was grateful to God for allowing me this momentous moment. Her brokenness led to both of us receiving some well-deserved healing.

Over the years since, I realized that my forgiveness for her doesn't change everything overnight. Even though I forgave her, I still had haunting memories of the abuse. Forgiveness doesn't erase what happened. It doesn't erase the nightmares or long-lasting damage that resulted from her actions.

I was still a victim, but instead of dwelling on the pain and allowing it to continue to hinder my life, I allowed Jesus to help me with this battle over my mind. I was free from the poison of bitterness.

Since I forgave my sister, we were able to start over in our relationship. We became friends. However, sometimes a simple hug could trigger unpleasant memories. I had to keep reminding myself that she was not the same person and that I forgave her. Healing didn't happen overnight. It's a process that develops over time, but my journey wasn't over. I still had another abuser in my life.

THE HOPE I HAD

I reflected on how my sister responded when I addressed the past and how it led to the fantastic miracle of forgiveness and healing between us. I had an idea and a powerful hope.

Perhaps, one day, when the time is right, I might have a similar heart-to-heart talk with my mother and let her know I remembered the past and how she treated me. Maybe, just maybe, she will feel the same shame in her behavior. Perhaps, after all these years, she will tell me she's sorry.

Oh, if I could only hear those words from my mother's mouth coming from a heart of brokenness, remorse, and true repentance. Maybe she, too, thought I forgot about it, and she's too afraid to mention it to me. Perhaps I need to let her know that I still remember.

I suddenly realized that after all the abuse she's inflicted on me, I still desired to have a loving relationship with my mother. A chance to start over and maybe even become friends, like my sister and I did. If only she would humble herself and tell me she was sorry. Would that be so hard for her? That would mean she acknowledged her abuse, took responsibility for it, and regretted it.

Mother's Day wouldn't have to be so painful and awkward when picking out a Mother's Day card. Maybe phone calls to home wouldn't have to end in more insults, hateful words, and broken hearts. Her repentance could open a whole new beginning between us.

This new hope rose inside me, and I waited for the right time. But whenever I got near her, the opportunity never presented itself, just more pain, blame, and hate.

"JUST ACCEPT IT!"

Whenever I would visit home, I would try hard to keep our visit peaceful, but it always turned sour between Mom and me. She would always storm out of the room and slam doors to get away from me, or I would leave in a huff to keep from stirring up another fight between us.

My dad and sister would always apologize for her behavior. "Scott, I'm so sorry that she treats you like that. You did nothing to deserve it," they would say to me.

I always responded with the same question, "THEN

WHY DOES SHE DO IT? WHY DOES SHE HATE ME SO MUCH?"

"Your mother doesn't hate you; she loves you; she just doesn't know how to show it very well."

"That's not true. Mom doesn't treat either of you the same way she treats me. Why is it always just ME?" This question has haunted me for years.

"Scott, that's how your mother is. She's never going to change. You must accept that and forgive her. That's what Jesus would want you to do."

If I had a remote-control button, I would hit PAUSE right here to ponder what I just heard.

Really? That's what Jesus would want me to do? Just recognize that this is who she is, and this is just a part of her DNA? Am I just supposed to accept that and forgive her?

My dad and sister fed me this line of phony justification multiple times. They already accepted in their minds that Mom would never change. She would always be like this. The responsibility now fell on me to take her as she was. I should never expect her to change her practices and keep forgiving her, no matter what she does to me. No matter how much pain or suffering she causes me, accept it and keep forgiving her.

This attitude is the philosophy I have lived with and believed in for years. I'm a Christian, and this must be what is expected. Forgiveness. Seventy times seven. I learned to forgive my sister for her sins against me, and now I need to forgive my mother. So I prayed repeatedly to God, "I forgive her. Lord, help me stop hurting so much," and then I would put myself out there again and again. It became a vicious cycle of pain and abuse.

Every time I would leave her house, I felt wounded all

over again, and my heart was in pieces. I would sit in my car and marvel in stunned silence at how mean and cruel a mother could be towards her son. Then, out of anger and hurt, I vowed she would never hurt me anymore because I would never come around again. And then the struggle would start all over again.

"But I'm a Christian. I need to forgive her and accept her unconditionally." That's what Dad and my sister said. That's what the Pastor said. Isn't that what Jesus said? Forgive all those who trespass against me? If I don't forgive them for their trespasses against me, God won't forgive me for my trespasses against him. It's that simple. Just forgive her and love her, despite her hate and constant abuse.

This life for Jesus is much more complicated than I ever thought. It's hard. I don't know if I can keep doing this. No wonder so many people get hurt and wounded and decide to leave the church. Forgiving her is almost impossible to do. How often can I keep putting myself in the same position so she can hurt me again? Is it worth it? Do I even care anymore?

If only, just once, I could hear my Mom say to me, "I'm sorry."

If only.

9

THE SECOND CONFRONTATION

I n early 2014, I found myself back in south Louisiana, visiting again. As always, I dreaded going by to visit my family. Dad and my sister begged me to come and see them, but I knew that always meant seeing Mom. I started to keep my family away because I never wanted them to see the wicked ways of my mother. They stayed with my wife's family while I went alone to see my Dad and sister.

It was a bit later in the evening, but I mustered all the strength I had left and went. Mom had been sick recently, complaining of pain in her back and chest. She and my sister were not in the best physical health. As I visited with Dad and my sister, she lay reclined in her chair, listening but remaining mostly silent on her part. As long as she remained silent, I could enjoy my visit.

Dad finally needed to go to bed, and after hugging me and bidding his farewell, he retired for the night. I was finishing a conversation with my sister about my parenting experiences with my two daughters, and Mom started injecting more into the conversation. It was turning out to be an enjoyable visit for a change.

"I feel so blessed that Suzanne and I were able to home-school both our girls," I said as I tried to wrap up the long topic.

My sister agreed, "Yes, you both did a wonderful job with them. Your girls will never know what we had to experience back in the day."

Mom chimed in again. "You both went to public school, and it didn't kill you."

My sister quickly agreed, "Yes, Mother, but Scott and I were already perfect." She joked sarcastically and laughed.

Mom didn't find it humorous. "Neither of you was perfect, but I raised you both right." When I heard her speak those words, it hit me fast and hard. In my head, I could hear a voice screaming at me, NOW...THIS IS THE TIME! She seems to be in a decent mood; Dad's in bed; it's just us; go ahead, make your move.

Without hesitating, I blurted out, "Well, Mom, I don't remember it quite like that."

Did I say that? Am I going to do this here and now? Do I quickly bow out and change the subject, or will I go ahead and commit to this right now? My sister shot me a shocked look.

My mother raised her head in my direction. "What do you mean?"

I heard myself swallow hard. The room became deathly quiet. "Well, I don't remember you raising me the right way as you claim you did. I remember it being a little more different."

Mom's face became very hard, but she maintained her calm tone. "And just how do you remember it?"

"I remember the things you did to me growing up. I never forgot." It felt so surreal that I was saying these words to my mother. Hearing them coming out of my mouth felt like it wasn't happening. I had dreamed about having this conversation with her for years, and now without planning, it was happening.

"What things?" she demanded.

I'm going for it. I've never come this far before. I'm going to do this. "I remember all the times you used to beat and abuse me when Dad was traveling. I remember how you were always angry with me and would tell me how you never wanted me and that I was the antichrist and a mistake. I remember all the hateful words you said to me during my childhood. I never forgot any of it."

"I didn't do any of that. You're lying." She said rather calmly and quickly.

"No, Mom," my sister spoke up and quickly came to my defense. "He's right. You did do those things. I remember them, too. I had to pull you off of him several times. He's not lying."

The room became very cold and very silent. Maybe Mom thought she could convince me that none of it ever happened, but she didn't count on my sister speaking up and taking my side.

She turned her eyes toward the floor, and I could almost see the wheels spinning in her head. Was this going to be the moment I had dreamed about? This silence was the same type my sister displayed before she broke down and repented. I held my breath and waited. I watched.

Mom kept staring at the floor in total silence. Oh God, what's happening in that mind of hers? Am I finally going to hear those simple little words I had longed to hear? Come on, Mom, it can't be that hard. Just look me in the eye and say, "I'm sorry." Those two little words can change everything. I can forgive you; please say it, and we can start all over.

She finally laid her head back down on her recliner and took a breath to speak. I watched her lips and waited in anticipation of what she was about to say. It felt like forever. "Well..." she paused briefly and then blurted out, "...you deserved it!"

Silence. It was as if the earth had stopped moving for a moment. I couldn't breathe. Wait. Did she say that? Did I really hear those words come out of her mouth? Did she seriously reach down in the bottom of her soul after being confronted by her children accusing her of child abuse and respond with "You deserved it!"

The words hit my gut hard. It felt like a sack of bricks just punched me in my stomach. You could wrap up every beating Mom gave me as a child, every word of hate, every punch, and every slap across my face into one painful blow; it wouldn't have hit me as hard as those three little words just did. "You deserved it!" I can still hear her voice saying those words to this very day.

I sat there in total shock. This response was not what I expected to hear. Instead of taking advantage of the situation and apologizing for what she did to me, Mom finally acknowledged it. She said I actually deserved it. It almost sounded as if she was proud of what she had done. No regrets. Almost as if the opportunity presented itself, she would do it all over again and not change a single thing. How is this even possible? How can a grown woman who confesses to being a Christian sit here and conjure up the nerve to say something like that?

I finally worked up the strength to respond. "No, ma'am. No child deserves what you did to me."

"Well, you did," she said coldly.

I stood up. "It's getting late; I'm leaving." And with that, I grabbed my things and left as fast as possible. I was not about to sit there and give her the satisfaction of seeing me break down and cry. I fought back my tears long enough to say goodnight to my sister, who looked at me and mouthed "I'm sorry" behind my mother's back. My mother just sat there with her eyes closed. She was refusing to say anything else.

The next thing I remember, I was sitting alone in the darkness of my car. I was too shocked to cry. I just sat there. Her words echoed in my mind. "Well, you deserved it." Over and over again until the shock wore off, only to be replaced by heavy sobs. I cried all the way home, where my wife was waiting for me. I recounted the entire experience with her and cried some more.

That was the night my mother died. Oh, she continued to live and breathe in the physical sense, but she was no longer my mother. I never had a mother. She suddenly became "That Woman." She's that woman Dad called his wife. She's that woman my sister called her mother. But to me, she will forever be known as "That Woman"!

I vowed to be respectful towards her if I should ever see her again, but I would not hug or offer any loving terms of endearment as her son. I had to set some boundaries between us. Perhaps she will notice my cold reaction to her. Maybe she'll recognize how much her words hurt me when she said that.

I doubt it. Nothing but ice runs through Mom's veins. A

cold heart like hers will never feel remorse, and a hard soul will never consider anyone else's feelings.

10

———————

THE FINAL COUNTDOWN

About three months later, I was at home in Mississippi and received a phone call from Dad. He told me Mom was in the hospital with severe back pain and upper respiratory issues. I offered polite condolences and asked him to keep me posted.

Dad did not know about my previous conversation with Mom or the boundaries I had created to protect myself. I saw no advantage in telling him. It would only stir up more turmoil.

About three days later, my sister called. It was September 23, my parent's 52nd wedding anniversary. "I was calling to tell you that Dad went to see Mom today, and they renewed their wedding vows in the hospital."

"Oh, that's nice. I hope Dad's happy." It was the best I could muster on the spot, and I meant it. I want nothing but happiness for him, and if they are at a place where they can renew their wedding vows to each other, then good for them.

She continued, "Right after they renewed their vows, the doctor came in." She became very silent.

"Okay, what did he say?" (I hate having to pry information out of people.)

"The doctor said that Mom has cancer." She paused again to let those words sink in.

"Seriously? Cancer?" I asked, wondering if I heard that correctly.

"Yes, he said it's already in stage four, and they're talking about setting up hospice care for her." She started crying.

"Hospice? Already? Did they give her a time limit?"

"No, I just got back from being with her."

"How is she taking it?" I found myself suddenly caring, which was very unexpected.

"She says she already knew it was cancer, and she's ready to go."

After another moment of silence, I responded, "Okay, I'll pack a few things together and come into town. I can be there by 9:00 pm." I will attempt to lay aside my differences with her and offer support to the family during this difficult time. It's just the right thing to do.

"Wait," she added.

"Why? What's wrong?"

"I told Mom I was going to call you and fill you in and..." she paused, "she said no. She didn't want me to call you. She doesn't want you to know about it."

"What? She doesn't want me to know? Mom gets diagnosed with stage four cancer, and she doesn't want her son to know about it?"

"I know, Scott. I told her you had a right to know, regardless of how she felt about you."

"And?"

"She still told me not to tell you. I only called because I

knew she was wrong. She's still your mother, and you DO have a right to know."

"Thanks. Then I won't come. I'll wait until she's ready to tell me, if she ever lets me know. Thanks for calling and telling me."

"I'm so sorry, Scott. I'll keep you posted."

"Thanks." I hung up and contemplated what I had just heard. It felt like another slap to the face. How am I supposed to process this information? My mother is dying of cancer and doesn't want me to know about it. She has a death sentence hanging over her, and in her last days, she continues to keep me at arm's length. What did I ever do to deserve such hatred? Such bitterness? Wow. Just wow. How do I even respond to this?

I walked away and shared the news with my wife. We both sat there in stunned silence, pondering the reality of her situation.

It was only three short hours later when the phone rang again. I saw my sister's name flash across the caller ID. Oh great, more bad news. I clicked the call accept button, "Hey, what's up?"

My sister could hardly speak. Between the heavy sobs and shrieking, I could finally determine what she was trying to say. "MOM'S GONE. SCOTT, SHE'S GONE!" That's all she could say before she broke down into hysterical crying and weeping.

After a moment of shocked silence, I muttered, "I'll be there as fast as possible." And then I hung up.

It's over. Mom's gone. I went numb. Did I hear my sister right? Yes, I did. She said Mom's gone. She's really gone. Once the reality of what I heard hit me, I fell to my knees and started crying.

Why was I crying? This reaction to her death shocked even me. Was I weeping tears of grief because she was gone? Would I miss her? I had to stop and ponder this very question. Where were these tears coming from that flooded down my face? And then I realized why.

I'm not crying because I'm going to miss her. I'm crying because now that she's gone, so are my hopes and chances of ever establishing a proper mother/son relationship with her. My hopes have just died, right along with her bitterness and hatred. Now I'll never have a mother. And with that heavy revelation, I cried even harder.

THE LAST GOODBYE

The next day I was in town with my dad and sister. They displayed an expected amount of grief over her passing. I tried but had no more sorrow to bear. My dad and sister made all the arrangements. There would be no funeral, no memorial, just a cremation. How fitting.

She had no friends outside a few Facebook connections from across the country who only knew her online. How easy is it to appear loving when you can hide behind a screen name and avatar? Several of them posted how they would miss her encouraging posts, loving support, and random acts of kindness.

I found out she was making handmade blankets for her online friends and sending them out for birthdays and baby gifts. Who was this woman they spoke so fondly of? Sadly, I never met her. Perhaps we're thinking of two different people.

I needed to see her one last time before they cremated her body. I needed to see "That Woman" that gave birth to me and called herself my mother. So I asked for that moment alone with her.

My sister went in first to say her last goodbye. I could hear her crying inside, so I walked further down and waited. Finally, she came out with her hands full of soaked tissues. She passed by me and nodded that it was my turn. I took a deep breath and went inside.

I gently closed the door behind me, turned around slowly, and saw her body on a cold metal table, lying naked under a white sheet draped over her. Her hair hung straight down, still wet and stringy from being washed. That stiff body was all that remained of my mother. I stood there, taking it all in. And then I walked closer to her.

I looked down at her, trying to find the woman I once knew, but all I saw was a corpse that resembled my mother. I reached out and touched her cheek with the back of my hand. It was cold. Dead cold.

"Why?" The question came out of my mouth with no hesitation. "Why did you hate me?" I waited, almost expecting an answer. "What did I ever do to make you hate me so much?" Then I stood there, looking at her in awkward silence. Her voice echoed in my mind, "You deserved it!" All the pain from those words came rushing back to me.

I turned and headed towards the door. Before I walked out, I turned once again in her direction, gave her one last glance, and offered my final words, "At least you'll never be able to hurt me again." And then I walked out.

11

THE AFTERMATH

Over the next couple of years, I repeatedly pondered my relationship with my mother and questioned my ability to forgive her. It's not like I will ever see her express remorse for how she treated me or repent of the abuse she inflicted upon me.

I will never hear her say those two brief words, "I'm sorry." Instead, all that keeps replaying in my mind is the unexpected memory of her words, "Well, you deserved it." It might as well be the last thing she ever said to me because I can't remember anything else after that. I might have seen her again after that night, but it was cold, and we had nothing to say to each other.

Forgiving my sister's abuse was much easier. How do I know I forgave her? Because I could visit with her and not feel disgusted like I once felt when she abused me or in the years that followed. I saw the fruit of her repentance displayed in her life, and she continued to grow in her relationship with Christ. Yes, sometimes the memories still haunt me. Still, I must keep reminding myself how she repented, how she isn't the same person anymore, and how I forgave her.

Funny how after Mom passed away, my visits home became much more pleasant. I didn't fear hurtful words or hateful actions. I could finally leave feeling good about our visit.

Several times, my sister would share with me how she missed Mom and could still feel Mom's presence in the house with her. My sister still held onto her ashes and couldn't bring herself to bury them. She was always looking at photos of Mom and telling me how hard it was for her to accept her passing.

I confessed I could not share the same grief. My mourning differed from hers because of the abuse. I couldn't share the same feelings about missing Mom; my sister understood my conflict and didn't make me feel guilty. She accepted that she and I had an utterly unconventional relationship and experience with our mother.

We finally got around to discussing that final conversation mom had with me. "Scott, I'm sorry Mom treated you the way she did."

"Me too. I wish I understood why she did it."

My sister paused and looked away for a moment. "I think I know why."

I quickly glanced up from the TV. "Why?" Now she had MY full undivided attention.

After a brief pause, she tried to change the subject. "Can you hand me the remote control to the TV? I can't hear it."

"Yes, I can, but why?"

"Why what?"

"You just said you know why she treated me the way she did."

She paused again, searching for the right words, and then continued, "Mom went through a few years where she was addicted to narcotics and had to go into rehab to get clean. She wasn't herself, and she did things she later regretted."

"I already know that, but the narcotics aren't the reason she treated me that way."

"How do you know?"

"Because she wasn't always using and still treated me that way. And when she was addicted, she never treated you or anyone else the same way, only me. She only directed her hate and abuse toward me. So it goes much deeper than just a narcotic addiction."

My sister sat back quietly in her chair as she pondered my words. I examined her facial expression and could tell she wanted to say something else. "What is it?" I asked.

"What?"

"What are you not telling me?"

"Nothing, I promise you. If there were anything else to share, I would." I knew she was not telling me the truth. I could tell there was a reason. Whatever it was, I could tell she was trying to protect me from knowing the whole truth. Maybe not tonight, but eventually, I will find out.

DECLINING HEALTH

My sister and father's health continued to decline. Since I was in Mississippi, they depended on and cared for each other. Still, for the things they couldn't do, they had Samantha, a hired help who came in once or twice a week, cooked some meals, did some light cleaning, and washed some clothes. She was so helpful in their season of need, and for my sister, she became a trusted and faithful friend. Every chance she got, my sister would share her faith with Samantha.

I was always thankful for Sam, and every time I met or talked to her on the phone, I shared my gratitude for her dedication, hard work, and friendship with them. She became an extended member of the family.

My sister's health seemed to decline faster than my father's. Several times, she developed infections that landed her in the emergency room for several days at a time. Between her COPD, kidney problems, deteriorating bone disease, and diabetes, she became a regular in the emergency room and hospital.

Sometimes, if Sam wasn't available, I had to come into town and take care of Dad while my sister recovered. Dad was barely walking with his walker and was getting slower and slower. I couldn't decide who was worse off between her health and Dad's. They both maintained a fast and steady course downhill.

My sister developed an infection in her foot that landed her back in the hospital on her birthday. The doctors said the disease was severe and that they must remove her foot. I sat on the edge of her hospital bed and cried with her, and then we prayed. Her biggest concern was how she would care for our father if she lost her foot.

Over the next few days, her foot improved, and after another inspection, the doctors decided they could save her foot. Within days, she was back at home with Dad, recovering.

I went back to Mississippi, and Sam came over several times, assisting Dad and my sister in any way she could. We were all grateful for her help.

EASTER SUNDAY

It was Easter Sunday morning in 2022, and my sister was back in the hospital after what she thought was a stroke. I spoke to her on the phone before I started my Easter morning service, and she sounded confused and weak. It was difficult for her to talk with an air mask over her face, but she tried her best.

"How do you feel today?" I asked.

"I don't know."

"Can you move all your body parts?"

"Yeah."

"Good, that's a good sign."

"Hang on, Scott," she said as a nurse entered her room. I could hear the nurse speaking to my sister in the background, telling her that she could take a shower and wash her hair after breakfast. Hearing this was great news to me. She was doing much better than I thought. If she can get up and walk, she might return home to Dad soon.

"Okay, I'm back," she said, breathing slightly like Darth Vader.

"I have to go. It's about time for worship to start, but I'll call you after church to check on you. I just wanted to see how you were feeling."

"Thank you."

"Make sure you give someone at the nurses' station my phone number in case of an emergency."

"Okay, I will." I could tell she was struggling to talk.

"Happy Easter, and I love you very much."

"Happy Easter, and I love you, too," she said. I finally hung up, went into the sanctuary, and began our Easter service.

As I began my morning message, my phone quietly

vibrated on the pulpit. I continued preaching but tilted my phone slightly and recognized the number of the hospital calling. An icy chill ran through my spine, but I continued preaching.

After the service, I returned the call, only to find out that my sister had passed away. This time, I cried and knew where the tears were coming from. They were tears of remorse because I knew I would miss my sister, and that's how I knew I had forgiven her.

Oh, how different this experience was from my mother's death. Very different indeed.

I packed my bags and went home to tell my father that my sister, his daughter, was gone. That was the hardest thing I ever had to do in my life. Nothing could have prepared me for the reaction he had. I have never seen my father that heartbroken. From this point on, I was all he had left.

THE REVELATION

I ended up resigning from my position as pastor in Mississippi. I planned to move back home to south Louisiana to care for Dad. He was much too ill and depressed to participate in any funeral, so we did the same thing that we did for my mother. We had my sister cremated.

I told Samantha, their caregiver, how much I appreciated her loyalty and faithfulness to my sister and Dad. She expressed her joy over the years from getting to know them. Then she shared something with me that confirmed what I already knew.

She told me my sister confided about how my mother abused and mistreated me throughout my life. My sister felt so sorry because she knew Mom never wanted me.

Did I hear that right? She just said my mom never wanted me. My sister must have told her that. When I heard Samantha say those painful words, it hit me like the missing piece of a puzzle.

After Mom had my sister, she was ready to move on with her life, but I came along. I was a mistake. Her pregnancy with me was an interruption of her plans, her dreams, and her goals. That's why she rode the horse again. She fell off, hoping the fall would cause another miscarriage, but she didn't expect me to survive. Then, when I was born, I was the wrong sex, and all her hopes of wealth and security failed.

Since she became pregnant with me, I was nothing more than an interruption and an unexpected burden to her. Because of me, she lost her horse and all her dreams. I was a constant living reminder to her of what she had lost. Now it all made sense to me. It was just as Samantha said. My mother never wanted me.

This reality must be what my sister wanted to tell me but didn't. She knew why Mom treated me the way she did, but she didn't want me to understand why. She was protecting me. But I already knew it, and hearing Sam say those very words only confirmed it for me.

I felt a mixed bag of emotions. On the one hand, it's hard to learn that your mother never wanted you. Your very exis- tence caused her depression and failed opportunities. But none of that was my fault. I didn't ask to be born, and even though Mom might have considered me a terrible mistake, God had a divine plan and purpose for my life. Before I was even born, He already had my life mapped and planned out for me.

People might make mistakes, but God doesn't. I don't believe it's my fault that Mom never saw past her selfishness and misery of an unexpected pregnancy. She never saw and accepted me as a blessing from God.

I no longer believe that it's my fault, after all. I don't have to carry that guilt anymore. Mom not wanting me wasn't MY burden to bear; it was hers, and she held it to the very bitter end. Instead of feeling angry about how she treated me, I now felt sorry for her because she was so miserable. This misery happens when people choose to live life as a victim of their past. She lived her life as a victim of her own mistakes; sadly, that was her choice.

But it's not my choice; I no longer have to be a victim. I chose to be free.

12

CLOSURE

I have often thought about my father's reaction to me telling him about my mom's abuse of me as a child. I have often wondered why he never did anything to stop it. He knew what she was doing to me while he was gone and witnessed her mistreating me as an adult. He has tried several times to apologize on her behalf, but that was never his responsibility or place to speak for her.

I still can't wrap my mind around his philosophy of forgiving, forgetting, and accepting her as she is without expecting any changes from her. All he wanted was peace, and since she wasn't going to change, the expectation fell on me to overlook her abusive words and behavior and forgive her.

I've never doubted my father's love for me, but now as an adult, these questions have haunted me about his perspective on the whole issue of my abuse.

Since Mom has been gone for several years now, he has commented many times how much he regrets traveling as much as he did and leaving me alone with her. He knows I'm damaged and still struggling with memories and pain from her abuse.

I've shared my story with a few close friends, and many have questioned my reaction to my father's lack of protection. They see him as being just as guilty for not stopping it. As an adult, I can look back and see their perspective, and they're right. I have every right to be offended, hurt and angry towards him for leaving me to her abuse. But I'm not for some strange reason that I can't explain.

I can easily hold him accountable for his terrible choices and how I have suffered because of his lack of protection, but what good would that do me now or him?

I can easily attempt to justify his poor choice, like he needed to keep his job to pay the bills and had no other option. But that doesn't justify leaving a child alone with an abuser. The harder I try, the more I realize there isn't any justification for what he did, and yet, I'm not angry with him. Knowing he regrets leaving me alone with her now is enough for me.

All I can remember is how I looked forward to him coming home, spending time with him, and the few short days of rest I had from Mom's abuse.

He's a man with many faults, but I still love him and never thought of him as responsible for her actions. Maybe that's simple forgiveness talking, being able to overlook his failures. Perhaps I've learned more about forgiveness than I realized.

ANOTHER SETBACK

Dad was now living alone, and I was busy wrapping up my duties at the church, packing, and preparing to move to

Louisiana. I called twice a day and had my daughter and friends going by and checking on him daily. Meals were being prepared for him until I could make my move, but since my sister passed away, his health declined even faster, and he lost his ability to walk.

I stopped everything I was doing and rushed back down to Louisiana. His color was pale, and he had no strength left. He thought he was dying and wouldn't make it till morning. I immediately called for an ambulance, and they came and carried him to the emergency room. They examined him, and he suffered from dehydration, was extremely malnourished, and had very low blood sugar—all typical of a man suffering from depression.

He stayed in the hospital and slowly improved, but he still couldn't walk. Since I knew he was in good care for a few days, I went back to Mississippi, finished packing everything up, and prepared to move to Louisiana.

ASHES TO ASHES

It was a very stressful season of transition for Suzanne and me. There was so much happening all at once. Suzanne and I had to quit our jobs and move our stuff into storage in Lafayette. We had to check on Dad daily and plan to transfer him into a physical therapy facility. We still had his two dogs to care for and cleaned my sister's belongings out of his house. We still had to carry out having her body cremated and closing her online business and personal affairs. It all became overwhelming for us.

As we were cleaning out my dad's house, I found my mother's ashes. My sister refused to part with them and kept them close to her. Now I had two sets of ashes in my dad's house—my mother's and my sister's, side by side. Just as they would have wanted it. Dad said it was too painful to see them, and I sure didn't want to keep them, so I decided I needed closure.

With Dad's permission, I scheduled a small family gathering with only my loving wife, my two beautiful daughters, my fantastic son-in-law, and my handsome new grandson. Our dear friends, my daughter's pastors, lovingly offered to lead us in a small ceremony at my grandparents' graveside at the cemetery. After the brief ceremony, I planned on sprinkling my mom's and sister's ashes over my grandparents' grave. I knew my mother would have wanted it this way.

That morning, as I was getting dressed for our family service, I thought about what I was about to do, and a fantastic revelation hit me. I stood up, and tears ran down my cheek as I realized what was happening.

Here I was, preparing to put to rest the ashes of the two people who hurt me the most in my life while being surrounded by the people who love me the most, my family and friends.

What irony! What a fantastic thing I was experiencing! I suddenly realized that despite all the pain and abuse these two people inflicted on me over the years, God had been so gracious by providing me with a loving wife and family. Suzanne was more than just my best friend; she was my soulmate who loved and accepted me with all my struggles and insecurities.

I also recognized my blessing in my two beautiful daughters, Jessi and Victoria. They loved and cared for me, no matter how twisted or dysfunctional my childhood was. They didn't see me as a victim; they saw me for who I became, despite my past.

And now, I have a fantastic son-in-law, Seth, who is also a minister and a man of God, whom I love and treat as my son and who has given me my first grandchild, my sweet, handsome little man, Jackson.

After being rejected and abused for so many years, I realized and acknowledged that God had provided me with the most wonderful and loving family any man could ask for. During one of my life's most difficult days, they stood by my side, supporting and encouraging me.

One chapter of my life was indeed closing. However, I had another chapter of my life standing beside me, still being written. This chapter is the one that matters the most now.

Whatever happened in my past doesn't matter anymore because I still have a future. I refuse to live my life as a victim of my past as my mom did. I refuse to be identified by my abuse. I choose instead to be recognized as a child of God, set free from the bondage of pain and insecurities.

I still have some scars to remind me of what I experienced. Still, instead of crying over my past and hiding my scars in shame, I can show off my scars as a reminder and testimony of what God brought me through.

I may still have some cracks and some healing to do in my life, but now I'm confident that God will be faithful to complete the work He has started in me. Thank you, Jesus, for revealing how blessed I am.

That day, I got to close the book on my past and open a new door to my future, which is in Christ Jesus. Now it's time to dig deep into my heart and begin the journey of forgiveness.

PART II

THE JOURNEY OF FORGIVENESS

13

PREPARING FOR THE JOURNEY

In introducing this book, I described some genuine and raw emotions about the difficulty of forgiveness. The feelings are real. Forgiving someone for offending or abusing you can be one of the hardest things a Christian or non-Christian can do.

Why is it so hard? Because you're hurting and wounded. There was a significant act of injustice inflicted upon you. Regardless of the intent, forgiveness can be challenging if you are a victim of any offense or abuse. Sometimes, it can feel simply impossible.

But then Jesus says clearly in Matthew,

"For if you forgive other people when they sin against you, your heavenly Father will also forgive you. But if you do not forgive others their sins, your father will not forgive your sins." (Matthew 6:14-15)

What a sobering scripture. I believe it's saying our forgiveness from God depends on our ability to forgive others who sin against us. It sounds effortless, but when we are still nursing our fresh wounds and trying to heal from our abuse, it's not as easy as it sounds when someone says, "Forgive them."

70 X 7

Let us return to the passage of scripture that this book began with, in Matthew 18. Peter, the disciple who seemed to get into a lot of trouble, went to Jesus one day and asked him, "How many times should I forgive my brothers or sisters who sin against me? Seven times?"

This question was honest. Peter already knew that the Jewish rabbis taught that forgiving someone over three times was unnecessary. They used the example of Amos 1:3-13, when God forgave Israel's enemies three times before passing judgment on them.

But before going into Jerusalem, Jesus taught the disciples, *"If your brother or sister sins against you, rebuke them; and if they repent, forgive them. Even if they sin against you seven times in a day and seven times come back to you saying 'I repent,' you must forgive them." (Luke 17:3-4)*

From the question Peter asked Jesus, I suspect Peter might have had some issues with some of the other disciples. They spent much time together, traveling, sleeping, working, ministering, cooking, cleaning, and serving others side by side.

This lifestyle reminds me of my time in Bible school, where the same group of students surrounded me daily for an entire year. Sure, we loved each other, studied, ministered, and worked together. Still, when you spend that amount of time around the same group of people daily, there's bound to be some personality clashes.

These men that Jesus hand-selected to follow him were no different. They were a motley crew of fishermen, a tax collector, a political zealot, and a thief. These are not the type of men traditionally known to hang together in the same social circles. They couldn't be more different from each other. The only thing they had in common was they were all sinners saved by grace, except for Judas, who was a thief and betrayed the Lord. There were bound to be some personality clashes among them.

I can imagine Peter was reaching his limit with some of them. Peter already heard Jesus teach about forgiving your offenders seven times a day. Still, even he might have wondered if there was a limit to forgiving these morons for their consistent offenses against him.

I supposed Peter was hoping it was only seven times. Maybe once he fulfilled his forgiveness quota of seven, he would finally be justified to seek some well-deserved revenge on his offenders. But before he opens that can of "Whoop Rump" on them, he better double-check with Jesus to confirm that the total number of forgiveness expected from him is only seven.

Jesus must have chuckled at Peter's question and took a little delight in correcting him. "I tell you, not seven times, but seventy times seven." Oh, how I wish I could have seen Peter's face at that moment. Peter was thinking about the law, but Jesus' response went beyond the traditional Jewish law and promoted a much better law of grace and mercy.

Now, if we were to take Jesus' response 70 x 7 literally, the total number of times to forgive others would add up to 490 times. Most bible scholars agree that this is a metaphor, meaning that our forgiveness should permanently abound in grace and never cease. It should not just stop once we reach the magic number, 490 times. Doing this would require a proper record book of offenses.

Jesus emphasizes several times in scripture how important it is that we love one another. It's the second greatest commandment, just short of loving God with all our hearts. 1 Corinthians 13 is the love chapter. It contains the biblical definition of perfect love and describes how God expects us to love one another.

Paul said, *"Love is patient, love is kind. It does not envy, it does not boast, it is not proud. It does not dishonor others, it is not self-seeking, it is not easily angered, it keeps no record of wrongdoings." (1 Corinthians 13:4-5)*

If we had to count how many times we offered forgiveness to someone who offended us, we would go against this scripture that describes love as *"keeping no record of wrongdoing."* Therefore, keeping count of one's offenses until we hit the magic number of seven or 490 would be completely unbiblical.

THE LIST

I recently discovered that someone in my church kept a recorded list of everything they perceived I was doing wrong as a pastor. As long as they kept that list, they kept their eyes open and watched every little thing I did, eager to find something else and add it to their growing list.

I suppose it helped them justify why they set themselves up against me. But it didn't take long for that person to realize that as long as they kept that list and kept searching for new things to add to it, the more miserable they became. Thankfully, after some time, they threw their list away.

Paul clearly said that love is *"keeping no record of wrong."*

You know, this is much harder than it sounds. Some of us may not be keeping a written journal of our enemies' wrong-doings. Still, whenever people offend us, we are quickly reminded of all the times when they did the same or similar things. We have a mental record and haven't forgotten what the offender did. This offense is just another offense upon a complete history of despicable acts. In our minds, it keeps building and building until one day, we can't take it anymore, and we explode in a rage of anger, tears, or both.

I counseled a married couple once who was on the brink of divorce. By the time the couple came before me, they already had it in their minds that they couldn't live with each other any longer. Every little thing each did would aggravate the other, and there seemed to be no compromise or compassion left.

They each laid out their case against the other, and out of respect, I listened. Most of the time, people just want to be heard and have their frustrations and complaints acknowl-edged. That alone can bring an incredible amount of healing.

When I listened to their list of complaints against each other, each item they laid out seemed so petty on the surface. As I listened, I noticed the offenses increased from little irritations to deep hurts and insecurities that they never communicated to each other. These severe issues will become the rich soil for more minor and insignificant seeds of offense. They will take root and grow into thick vines and branches that can choke the life out of a marriage.

Once we addressed the more profound issues between them and the lack of communication, it opened a new door of discovery for them. They shared their hearts and listened to each other for the first time. Once there was an understanding between them, the petty things took care of themselves, and they gained a new outlook and respect for each other.

It helps when we allow the Holy Spirit to deal with our hidden pain and emotions. We must learn to communicate what's happening in our hearts and listen to what the Lord says. Once we do, we discover the fullness of His healing and restoration.

But when we allow our pain and insecurities to fester without adequately dealing with them, we will only toil the soil and make it fertile for the seeds of offense to grow. They will finally develop into vines and branches that will choke the life and joy out of our lives.

HOW?

I did not know how to deal appropriately with my abusers or tell someone I needed help. Each offense became another seed that grew into another thick vine that choked me.

I tried so hard to do the right thing and forgive my abusers. If I could do what the pastor said, "Love and forgive your enemies," I wouldn't have to carry this heavy load or suffer the consequences of my abuse. As long as I held on to the pain and bitterness, I risked not being forgiven by God. I will be forever drowning in a sea of bitterness and unforgiveness.

I repeatedly prayed, "Lord, take this pain away from me so I can forgive them. Once it stops hurting, will I be able to forgive them then? How can I simply offer forgiveness to the person who offended and abused me when that person stole so much from me and left me so shattered and in ruins? How can I just say, 'Here, I forgive you'? How do I do that?"

What if they don't even ask for my forgiveness? What if they don't even acknowledge their wrongdoing? I mean, isn't repentance a requirement for Jesus to forgive me of MY sins? I still have to confess my sins and repent for God to forgive me, so why doesn't my abuser have to repent and ask for my forgiveness? It sure would be easier.

It's an honest question. Some might consider the honesty of this question to be bordering on the side of blasphemy, but it's a real struggle. It's the same question I have struggled with for many years.

My mother never admitted or confessed to any wrong-doing on her part. She never repented, and she never asked for my forgiveness. How can I forgive that? My inability to forgive her had tormented me for so long. But it's because I didn't understand what forgiveness was.

My mom and sister aren't the only ones who ever offended or hurt me. People I have worked with, ministered with, and worshiped with have also taken advantage of me and left me wounded. Sometimes, when I see these people or even hear their names brought up in conversation, my mind automatically returns to the pain and offense they caused me. I feel horrible feelings in the pit of my stomach.

The original seeds of offense continued to grow into thick vines that were already choking me.

HIDDEN RAGE

Once, my wife and I were on vacation from pastoring and visiting my daughter Jessi in Louisiana. We drove around, ran errands, and enjoyed our time together.

We were approaching a hotel where I once worked as a server inside a restaurant. Every time I passed it, I thought of another chapter of pain in my life from years earlier.

The manager, who was once my friend, falsely accused me of working against him to get him fired so I could have his job, which wasn't true. I didn't want his career. But he was so insecure. He had no reason to fire me, so he joined forces with the head of human resources and tried to get me to quit, which meant several cruel acts of injustice and lies against me.

I was married with two children, so I couldn't afford the luxury of just quitting. I needed that job, so I had no choice but to accept and endure their unjust acts and accusations against me until I found another job.

As my daughter and I drove by the hotel that day, I glanced over at the hotel. That's when I saw the head of human resources walking across the parking lot. Immediately, my face heated with hot anger as it brought back all those memories and unpleasant feelings I had years before. I never properly dealt with it back then, and I did not know those feelings were still festering in me, growing deep roots.

When I saw him, I yelled, "THERE HE IS!" I pointed, "THAT ROTTEN PIECE OF $%@#!"

My daughter's eyes widened with shock. "DADDY!" she scolded. Immediately, I realized what I had said. "Where did THAT come from?" she asked.

I think I was just as shocked as she was by my very unexpected reaction. "Um, I don't know," I responded shamefully.

"I do," she said. "It came from your heart. It's good I'm driving; you would have gone back and run him over." We laughed, but she was right.

I did not know that much anger was still inside me, but when I saw him walking across the parking lot, I wanted her to turn the car around and run him over. I honestly hadn't considered him or my experience working there for a long time. Still, the very moment I saw him, it all came rushing back, and it filled me with a sudden desire to seek vengeance.

That happens when you don't deal appropriately with your anger against someone. You might move on and put it out of your mind, covering it up with busy activities and distractions, but somewhere deep inside, it's still there. It's brewing like hot lava in the belly of a volcano, waiting for just the right trigger to boil over and erupt, and when it does, it will show no mercy. It will choke the very life of everything God has planted inside your spirit like the seed sown along the path.

Listen to what the parable of the sower means: When anyone hears the message about the kingdom and does not understand it, the evil one comes and snatches away what was sown in their heart. This is the seed sown along the path. (Matthew 13:18-19)

We hear preachers preach about forgiveness all the time, and we think we understand it; but since we don't, we struggle with it. That's when the evil one comes along and snatches away the seed God sowed in our hearts.

IT'S COMMON

I'm not the only one who has ever struggled with this. Most of the pastoral counseling I've done involves people working on forgiving someone who abused or offended them.

If this is you, I have some good news. You're not alone. Sadly, it is much more common than you think. The church today struggles to heal from abuse of all kinds — physical, mental, and even sexual abuse — from trusted church leaders, loved ones, and even family members at home.

Sometimes, it seems like our abusers experience more grace than the victims do. Some people and churches take extraordinary measures to cover up and hide the offense and expect the victim to forgive and forget.

Many people do not understand forgiveness and have unrealistic expectations of themselves. When the victim cannot reach the expected level of forgiveness, he feels like he failed God. That's when we entertain giving up the fight, and once we give up the fight, Satan has won the war.

Through my study and experience with forgiveness, I'm ready to share some things I learned that have helped me, and I hope it can help you, too. Will you be able to forgive your offender after you read this? It all depends on your willingness to take this journey with me.

FINAL PREPARATION

Now, anytime my wife and I go on any trip or vacation, we spend a little time planning and preparing. My wife always lists things she needs to pack and checks off every item as she loads it. She's very organized and seldom ever forgets anything. She's always prepared and ready to focus on enjoying our vacation time.

As I think about it, I throw random stuff into my suitcase, hoping I have everything when I get to my destination. If either of us ends up forgetting anything, it's traditionally me. I then have to go out and buy whatever I forgot, which takes away from my ability to enjoy the vacation.

I have discovered that proper preparation before your journey can make the trip more fun. But very little planning and preparation can take time and pleasure away from the journey. Therefore, I encourage you, before you go any further into this journey of forgiveness, that you take a little time and reflect on your preparation.

Recognizing and confessing that you might need some help with forgiving someone is a beautiful first step. We cannot receive healing if we cannot admit and acknowledge that something broke inside us and that we need healing.

The hardest first step is confessing that we are victims, that some form of injustice committed against us has hurt and wounded us.

When I publicly announced on social media that I was writing a book on this topic, many friends and family reached out to me. They shared with me their own stories of abuse. For some, it was the first time they admitted it. When they learned I was also a victim, it gave them the confidence to come forward and tell me their stories.

I am more confident now that writing this book and sharing my story is what I'm supposed to do. There are so many more of us out there living in shame and fear, harboring secret pains and insecurities, and still struggling with how to forgive our abusers.

Before we go any further, let's take a moment to pray. Let's ask God to prepare our hearts and open our minds as we venture together on this journey of forgiveness.

"Heavenly Father, I acknowledge You today as the author and giver of all good things. You have extended Your arm of grace and mercy towards me once again. You have heard my cries and counted the tears of my broken heart. I thank You for loving me unconditionally and being ever so faithful to me, even when I haven't been faithful to You. I invite You to open my heart and understanding to discover what true biblical forgiveness is and what it isn't. Forgive me for my bitterness and for making excuses to justify my poor reaction to those who have offended me. Help me no longer live my life as a victim of my past. Help me embrace Your gift of healing and restoration. In Jesus' Holy and Precious name, Amen."

VERY TRULY I TELL YOU, YOU WILL WEEP AND MOURN WHILE THE WORLD REJOICES. YOU WILL GRIEVE, BUT YOUR GRIEF WILL TURN TO JOY!" (John 16:21)

14

BUSTING THE MYTH OF
FORGIVENESS

Sometimes we feel that forgiveness is impossible because we don't understand what forgiveness is. We have this idea that forgiveness is simply "letting go and letting God." It sounds nice on the surface. It always seems to incite a round of charismatic "Amens" whenever it's preached from behind the pulpit. But what does that even mean?

Some would explain it as letting go of our right to be offended and allowing God to change our attitude to gratitude. Can I be honest with you for a moment? Can we put aside all our theologies and be brutally honest? I want to barf every time I hear trite little religious answers like that. They sound spiritual and righteous, but it's not based on any real experience.

People mean well, but they don't know what they are saying or how ridiculous that sounds. Whenever I hear token comments like these, I bite my tongue, offer a polite thank you, and go my way before I say something I will regret later.

For me to share what forgiveness is, I find it easier to start by sharing what forgiveness is NOT! That way, we can remove all the unrealistic expectations out of the way. We can bust a few myths about forgiveness, focus on the real meaning and move on to our healing.

I. Forgiveness is NOT forgetting or pretending that the offense never happened.

"I forgive, but I won't forget." I've heard many pastors condemn statements like this because it sounds like someone is still harboring unforgiveness in their heart. They continue to preach: "If you cannot forget the offense, then you do not truly forgive it."

I'm not angry at these pastors; I consider them blessed that they never experienced abuse and never had to struggle with forgiving someone. No matter how hard you try, you will always have the memory of your abuse and pain.

Let's get real here. It happened, and it happened to you. No one should ever try to take that away or ignore your abuse. To expect you to pretend or act like it never happened and forget about it is lunacy.

Not only did the offense occur, but your resulting wounds and pain are real and justified. We are creatures of emotion. Our feelings are genuine, and we have no control over them. We might learn how to control our actions and reactions and suppress our feelings for a while, but we have no control over how we might feel when things happen, or people do things to us.

If you experience or witness something funny, you laugh. You can try to suppress it, but you still feel the emotion. Sometimes, I find humor at the worst times, during a funeral, or during a painful moment in someone's life. I try to be respectful by suppressing my laughter, but that isn't always easy. I can't help what I'm feeling.

If you see or experience something heartbreaking enough, you cry. You might hold back the tears and cover them up, but you can't turn off the feeling. If someone does or says something that makes you mad, you feel angry. If someone offends, abuses, or takes advantage of you, you can't help but feel hurt and wounded.

You might pretend it's all right and you're not hurt or offended, but inside, the pain is genuine. It's as natural as when our flesh breaks open and blood flows. It's a normal response to the wound. We cannot change the process of our emotions or what we feel.

In Psalm 56:8, David, who was called a man after God's own heart, expressed his emotions in song: *"Record my misery; list my tears on your scroll. Are they not in your record?"*

David knew God was aware of his pain; like David, God is also aware of our pain.

Forgiveness does not excuse the offense or ignore its consequences. Before we can offer forgiveness, we need first to acknowledge that the abuse took place and that it created pain in our lives.

Some people want to cover up their pain and pretend it isn't even there by saying, "I forgive you," and go along with their lives like it never happened. And then they wonder why the vines of bitterness are growing in their hearts and choking God's life out of them. It's like believing in God for healing but refusing to acknowledge that you're sick or wounded.

I knew a man who loved the Lord with all his heart but suffered shoulder pain from a previous injury. He was a man of faith who believed God would heal his shoulder supernaturally without the use of a doctor. Every time I saw him, I asked him how his shoulder was doing, and he always responded, "Oh, it's healed; nothing is wrong with it."

I always wondered how you could expect God to heal something if you can't even confess it's broken. I am also a person of faith, and while I believe in God's ability to heal anything, I first must admit that I'm wounded. Then I can believe God to manifest His complete healing.

Until the healing manifests, I can be authentic enough to respond to people, "It still hurts, but I still believe in God to heal it." Acknowledging the reality that something is broken or wounded takes nothing away from our faith in God's ultimate healing.

If anyone tries to tell you that forgiveness requires that you pretend that your offense never took place and you should "forgive and forget," don't fall for it. Otherwise, the pain will grow deep inside and take root, and you will continue to be hurt again and again.

For years, I thought forgiveness meant forgetting. Every time I did that and didn't hold my abusers accountable for their actions, I got hurt again.

It's years later, and I am just now permitting myself the right to acknowledge my abuse. I'm tired of pretending it never happened and that I'm okay because I'm not. There is damage and brokenness because of what they did to me. Painful memories and consequences still haunt me. No amount of forgiveness is going to take away the scars of my abuse. No amount of forgiveness is going to give back what they stole from me.

It's time to free yourself from hiding the truth and

acknowledge your wounds. Holding your abuser account-able for his actions and taking back your life is okay.

2. Forgiveness is NOT a free pass or a release from legal accountability.

FORGIVING PEOPLE of their offense or abuse does not erase their actions against you or release that person from legal responsibility. Some offenses against us are not only abusive but also criminal.

Laws protect and prevent innocent people from criminal actions and bring justice to those who have already committed them. When criminals break laws, there are consequences. Suppose criminals escape being held accountable for their crimes. In that case, they will be free to commit them again and again. They will leave behind a whole new crop of victims until someone holds them accountable.

It's possible to forgive people for their crimes against you. However, it still doesn't excuse or remove the conse-quences they brought upon themselves when they committed their crime.

It's also essential to note that when people commit a crime against you and you expose them for their abuse, the consequences are NOT your fault. It's common to be accused of an abuser's suffering because you refused to keep the abuse a secret.

Many times, when an abuser is brought to justice, he will suffer much more than just the legal consequences. Many of them suffer personal losses as well. They might lose their jobs, lose the trust and respect of their friends and family, and gain financial losses and difficulties.

What's important to remember is that it is NOT your fault. Your abuser risked these consequences when he committed his criminal action against you. You didn't ask for this and didn't bring it on. Let's not forget who the actual victim is here. Your abuser is only suffering the natural consequences of his own criminal choices.

Your part in exposing his abuse may prevent several other victims from being abused by the same offender.

If our legal system fails to hold him accountable for what he did to you, do not fear because he is still responsible to God for what he did. God will execute proper and perfect justice.

For we must all appear before the judgment seat of Christ, so that each one may receive what is due for what he has done in the body, whether good or evil.
(2 Corinthians 5:10)

But because of your stubbornness and your unrepentant heart, you are storing up wrath against yourself for the day of God's wrath, when his righteous judgment will be revealed. God will repay each person according to what they have done. (Romans 2:5-6)

Your abuser might escape the consequences of man's law. Still, there will come a day when he stands before God for his actions against you and suffers under God's perfect judicial system.

3. Forgiveness does NOT require trusting your offender again.

Suppose your abuser is someone you know already in your life: relative, friend, co-worker, church member, etc. You trusted him once but had that trust broken by an offense or an abusive action. In that case, you can still offer forgiveness without lowering your guard and trusting him again. The lack of trust is not a sign of unforgiveness.

You wouldn't trust a total stranger with your valuable or personal things unless you spent time with him, and he earned it by proving himself to you. We should be cautious before trusting someone who doesn't deserve it. Whenever that trust gets broken, it's not a simple thing to get back.

I have an excellent relationship with my father. He's the one person in my immediate family who never abused me. He always showed unconditional love in the best way he knew how. Did he make mistakes and poor choices? Absolutely, but he never intended to hurt or mistreat me.

About a year before I became a Christian, I experimented with my newfound independence during my teenage years of trying to find myself and discover who I was. I was lying to my parents about where I was and ended up going to places I shouldn't have gone, with people I should not have been with, and doing things I should not have been doing. Some would call this phase of teenage life the rebel phase.

I wasn't a bad kid; I was always respectful and didn't talk back to my parents. I wasn't always honest, and I got caught once or twice in a lie.

Mom was at work, and Dad received a tipoff from an

anonymous source one night that I was with some older people at a local nightclub.

Dad was waiting to confront me about my whereabouts when I got home. Before I could even think of an excuse or lie, he told me he already knew where I was. Then he looked me straight in the eye and said something I will never forget. "Scott, I will not punish you for lying to me about where you said you were going or being someplace you had no place being."

"You're not?" I asked in shock.

"No, but I can no longer trust your word to me. You lied, and it's going to be a long time before I can trust you again." And with that, he walked away and went to bed.

I stood there completely crushed as the reality of what I did set in. Losing my father's trust that night weighed heavier on me than any punishment or beating I could have received, and I deserved it. I deceived him and lied to get my way. He trusted me, and I took advantage of it. I was the offender that night, and even though he forgave me for my actions, I still lost his trust and had to work hard to regain it.

Forgiveness does not equal immediate trust. I know some wives who have lost faith in their husbands after being lied to, cheated on, and deceived. Of course, this happens in reversed roles as well, but my personal experience has been with men breaking trust with their wives.

When confronted and exposed for his deception, the husband would apologize, beg the wife to forgive him, and attempt to restore their marriage to the trust level they had before he lied. So many loving wives have forgiven their husbands, but they don't trust them right away. Trust must be earned again, and that can take some time.

I have seen some husbands attempt to turn the tide by

accusing their wives of not forgiving them because they don't trust them anymore. "If you truly forgive me, you will trust me again." This logic removes the consequences of their actions. It now places full responsibility on the wife to overlook what the husband did and treat him as if nothing ever happened.

This move is very selfish and manipulative. Narcissistic people are notorious for this defensive behavior and will use it to take full advantage of their wives.

Some trust levels may never be restored. We might never trust again a family member or adult who molests or abuses a child left in his care. With proper counseling, prayer, grace, and mercy, forgiveness might be available for the abuser. Still, that level of trust might be gone forever. This lack of faith is not a sign that forgiveness isn't available; it's a sign that there was a lesson learned and the same mistake will not be repeated.

So I repeat, forgiveness does not involve immediate trust.

4. Forgiveness does NOT require reconciliation with your abuser.

Reread number four until you comprehend what you just read. This point might be the most challenging truth to accept, but there's a vast difference between forgiveness and reconciliation.

Forgiveness is a personal decision to let go of your hatred and the right to seek vengeance or harm against your abuser. It's an act of faith. Now that you are releasing yourself from the responsibility of judging your abuser, it's in God's hands. God is far more capable of bringing perfect justice to your abuser than you are.

You can forgive your offender and still feel angry. You still might carry the pain and consequences of your abuse, but once you forgive him, it's no longer your offense to pass judgment on. You willfully give it to God to deal with now. That's where faith comes in.

Forgiveness also doesn't require repentance on behalf of your abuser, but it sure makes it more accessible. Forgiveness isn't about your abuser; it's about you. It's another step in the healing process. You can forgive someone and go about your way without facing that person again.

Reconciliation is something entirely different from forgiveness. Reconciliation is the restoration of friendly or loving relations between two people. For reconciliation to take place, it requires a desire from both the abuser and the victim to restore the brokenness that divided them.

The abuser must humble himself and take full responsibility for his actions and poor choices. He must not shift the blame or attempt to justify it; simply confess it and repent of it.

Healthy reconciliation between two people also includes a desire and promise to change their ways and do everything possible to keep that promise. This act is called repentance.

Once the offender repents and changes his ways, then it is up to the victim to offer enough faith to give the offender another chance. Reconciliation requires two people to make hard choices and come to an agreement together to restore their relationship. Reconciliation is a beautiful thing and a remarkable testimony to the restoring power of Jesus Christ.

However, if the abuser refuses to acknowledge and take responsibility for his offense, then reconciliation is not possible. The only option is to separate from the abuser until he is ready and willing to address the abuse. This separation is called setting boundaries to protect yourself.

Establishing boundaries is okay; just because you create boundaries doesn't mean you haven't forgiven your abuser. If you walk behind a horse and it kicks you, you might overlook the horse, but you also learn never to walk behind the horse. Lessons are learned. I have learned too late that forgiving my mother did not require me to let my guard down so she could continue to hurt me again and again. Drawing boundaries is not unforgiveness; it's simply using wisdom.

I've seen marriages broken apart by the actions of an unfaithful or abusive spouse. And while physical abuse isn't always the factor in the brokenness, emotional abuse can be just as damaging and painful. Until the cheating spouse is willing to take responsibility for his offense, boundaries might need to be drawn.

The victim can still offer forgiveness but not be expected to reconcile with the offender. Sometimes, no matter how much grace you offer people, they will still choose the path of abuse and offense. For some people, it's in their DNA to continue hurting and abusing people. It's called a sinful nature, and no amount of forgiveness on your part will ever change their ways.

As long as you have given your offense to God and forgiven your offender, you have permission to shake the dust from your feet and maintain your distance.

Whatever town or village you enter, search there for some worthy person and stay at their house until you leave. As you enter the home, give it your greeting. If the home is deserving, let your peace rest on it; if it is not, let your

*peace return to you. If anyone will not welcome you or
listen to your words, leave that home or town and shake
the dust off your feet. Truly I tell you, it will be more
bearable for Sodom and Gomorrah on the day of
judgment than for that town." (Matthew 10:11-15)*

5. Forgiveness does NOT bring instant healing.

If you should decide to forgive your offender, God bless you; you are strong and merciful. However, if you have expectations of instant healing from forgiving someone for offending or abusing you, you will be dreadfully disappointed.

But your feelings do not take priority over God's Word. Regardless of your emotions, God's Word still carries more weight and authority than your feelings.

*For if you forgive other people when they sin against you,
your heavenly Father will also forgive you.
(Matthew 6:14)*

Someone's abuse or offense has damaged you, which can seriously affect your feelings and emotions. Damage like that doesn't heal overnight just because you tell someone, "I forgive you." It may never leave you, but with God's help, forgiveness turns the open wound into scars; the scars are a consistent memory of the pain you experienced.

As you acknowledge God's constant presence in your life, you may never forget what happened. Still, you no longer feel the weight of your offense binding you and holding you hostage to shame like it once did.

Yes, it takes time. Forgiveness and healing are a journey, a process. Just like trust takes time to be restored, so will your spiritual health and well-being. There's light at the end of the tunnel, no matter how long or dark your tunnel is. Don't allow your feelings to deceive you and cause you to believe as though there's no hope available to you.

You're not the only one who's ever gone through that tunnel. Many have gone through it before you; sadly, many more will travel down that dark tunnel behind you. But place your hope in Christ Jesus, who promises to walk through that tunnel with us and not forsake us, even in the darkest places.

> *But those who hope in the Lord will renew their strength.*
> *They will soar on wings like eagles; they will run and not*
> *grow weary, they will walk and not faint."*
> *(Isaiah 40:31)*

15

WHAT IS FORGIVENESS?

Now that we have spent an entire chapter explaining what forgiveness is NOT, we can now remove all those unrealistic expectations out of the way and out of your life. Now it's time to explain what forgiveness is.

Psychologists define forgiveness as a conscious, deliberate decision to release your feelings of resentment or vengeance against someone who has abused or offended you, regardless of whether that person deserves it.

It's not a simple thing to come by, especially when all you've ever wanted to do is watch your abuser suffer and hurt as much as you have. Don't feel condemned if you've ever wanted to take justice into your own hands and harm the one who hurt you. It's normal.

Earlier, I said we are bodies with emotions and feelings we cannot control. Our emotions are like roller coasters, up and down every day, with unexpected twists and turns. Sometimes, our feelings are driven by hormones that seem to have a mind of their own. Other times, they are driven by situations outside our realm of control.

We can't depend on our feelings. They will deceive and lie to us, making us feel like we are in the depths of despair when, in reality, we're not, and everything around us is fine.

Take, for example, a woman experiencing postpartum depression after delivering her beautiful baby. It took her body nine months to prepare for delivery. After the baby is born, the hormones go into high gear, attempting to readjust to life.

The body will go through a whirlwind of emotions and feelings. Mom feels overwhelmed with joy one minute, and two minutes later, she's in a sobbing fit of frustration and anger.

The point is that our feelings are not to be trusted. We cannot allow our feelings to make life-changing decisions for us. Our feelings are not always an accurate reflection of reality.

We might feel justified in the flesh when we're angry and hurt when someone offends or abuses us. Our reaction to attack and hurt back is a natural reaction in the flesh.

We might want to treat our abusers like a glow stick, snap them in half, and shake their life out for the light to come on. This feeling we have to get even makes forgiving our abusers difficult.

We expect to stop feeling so angry and hurt before we can forgive. We're waiting until the pain stops and we no longer suffer the consequences before we can even think about saying, "I forgive you."

However, forgiveness is not a feeling; it's a choice we eventually must make despite how we feel. It's a conscious and deliberate choice we must subsequently make, despite how we feel inside. We must give up our right to pass judgment on our abusers and allow God to take it and deal with it according to His will.

If you're waiting for the pain to go away and to feel better before you forgive your abuser, you will be waiting for a very long time.

The memories and pain will always be there, and your feelings will draw you towards vengeance, wrath, and bitterness.

A HARD CHOICE TO MAKE

Satanists teach, "Do what thou wilt is the whole of the law," which means do whatever pleases you is the highest goal of the Satanist. Satan represents self-indulgence instead of abstinence or self-discipline.

You don't have to be a card-carrying member of the satanic church to live according to his commandments. You're already following his commandments whenever you live for yourself, doing whatever pleases you or allowing your feelings and emotions to dictate your actions.

But Luke records Jesus saying:

*Whoever wants to be my disciple must deny themselves
and take up their cross daily and follow me. For whoever
wants to save their life will lose it, but whoever loses their
life for me will save it.*
(Luke 9:23-24)

If we consider ourselves a disciple of Christ, then we

must lay aside our feelings and emotions. We must consider what God asks us to do with our anger and pain.

Here it is—the hard part. Jesus asks us to die to ourselves, take up our cross, and follow Him.

We are now facing a hard choice to make. Do we keep feeding our anger and pain against our abusers and allow bitterness and unforgiveness to take over in our lives? Or do we die to our flesh and trust God to deal with our abusers in any way he sees fit?

Will we "do what thou wilt" and enjoy the temporary satisfaction it brings us? Or will we choose the more challenging path, die to our flesh, and receive eternal life?

"But God, this is hard. Look what they did to me. I'm broken because of their selfishness and abuse."

"Yes, my child, I already know."

"But look, Lord, I still have all these scars because of them."

"Yes, and now look at my scars from when they crucified me. Here, place your hand on my side and feel the hole from when they pierced me."

"So you understand the pain from abuse, don't you?"

"Yes, my beloved, I do. I was beaten, laughed at, and mocked by my enemies. One of my followers, who sold me for 30 pieces of silver, betrayed me. All my friends abandoned me and left me to face my accusers alone. My closest friend even denied that he knew me. Yes, my child, I understand exactly what you are suffering from."

"Oh Jesus, I'm sorry. I keep forgetting about all the suffering you went through."

"I forgive you."

"Just like that, huh? Can you forgive me just like that?"

"It's because I love you."

"I love you too, Lord."

"If you love me, keep my commands. And I will ask the Father, and he will give you another advocate to help you and be with you forever — the Spirit of truth." *(John 14:15-17)*.

This truth is what it all comes to. Making the tough choice to let go of our right to pass judgment and trust God to take our pain and execute His judgment against my offender and abuser.

> *So I say, walk by the Spirit, and you will not gratify the desires of the flesh. For the flesh desires what is contrary to the Spirit, and the Spirit what is contrary to the flesh. They are in conflict with each other, so that you are not to do whatever you want. (Galatians 5:16-17)*

GOD'S JUSTICE IS BETTER THAN OURS.

When we dream of ways to bring suffering and vengeance to our abuser, we can be very dark and creative in our imagination. I often imagined placing super glue in my mother's shampoo and fart spray in her perfume. Some things we can imagine might bring a wicked little smile across our faces, but these thoughts and fantasies are not healthy for our spirits.

> *Finally, brothers and sisters, whatever is true, whatever is noble, whatever is right, whatever is pure, whatever is lovely, whatever is admirable—if anything is excellent or praiseworthy—think about such things. Whatever you*

have learned or received or heard from me, or seen in me
—put it into practice. And the God of peace will be with
you." (Philippians 4:8-9)

If we follow scripture, we must give up thinking and imagining dark and wicked things against our abusers. By choosing to forgive someone, we are giving up our right to pass judgment on the one who offended or abused us.

By doing this, we are not declaring that what our abusers did to us is okay or that we will simply ignore the damage or pain they caused us and pretend that it never happened.

We are not saying we will ever forget what they did to us.

We are not saying that we release them of all responsibility and legal consequences of their actions against us.

We are not saying we will trust them again with the same trust we once had.

We are not saying that we are reconciling ourselves back to them.

But what we ARE saying is, "I am trusting God by handing over my right to seek vengeance against them. I am no longer responsible for judging them or their abuse of me. I am releasing myself from this heaviness and trusting that God will take this from me and will become their judge. I am trusting that God's justice is perfect and righteous."

Suppose God should judge them and execute consequences against them for what they did to us. In that case, He will do a much better job than we could imagine. Our desire to see them suffer will no longer be our chain of bondage. God's justice is as perfect as He is.

HOWEVER, please pay close attention to what I am about to say.

Should God deal with our abusers for their sins against us and bring them to the point of brokenness and repentance, and He forgives them for their abuse against us, then we must be okay with that as well.

If we're going to trust God to deal with them His way, then we must accept that God still loves them just as He loves us, and His first desire is to see them come to repentance.

The Lord is not slow in keeping his promise, as some understand slowness. Instead he is patient with you, not wanting anyone to perish, but everyone to come to repentance." (2 Peter 3:9)

God is a loving and patient God. He desires every single sinner to come to the point of repentance and find forgiveness and salvation from his sins. While it may not seem fair to us that our abusers might repent and receive forgiveness from God, it's no longer our case to judge.

Forgiving our abusers is simply turning it over to God and allowing Him to do what's best for all of our lives. Whether it brings instant judgment or leads to their being forgiven by God, we must accept whatever happens and trust that it's done once we give it to God. It's over on our part. We have removed our hands from the situation.

THAT is forgiveness. When we offer forgiveness to our enemies, we're not presenting them with free passes. They may passionately want our forgiveness, thinking that once we forgive them, they are free of the consequences of their actions. Still, in reality, it's God's forgiveness they should be seeking.

Whether we forgive them does not erase their accountability to God for what they did to us. They cannot escape his judgment for their actions against us. Forgiving them is not about them or for them. It's about us. It's about letting go of the poison of hate and bitterness because it darkens our hearts and prevents us from experiencing God's supernatural grace and mercy for our sins.

16

THE POISON OF BITTERNESS

Whenever a poisonous snake attacks and bites its victim, it releases poison into the bloodstream. That poison contains hemotoxic properties that go to work immediately and attack the blood, causing the blood to thicken and clot. Unless medical assistance is received quickly, the venom of a snake will spread through the bloodstream and attack the heart, leading its victim to a quick and painful death.

Whenever we permit bitterness and hatred into our lives, that bitterness deposits a spiritual poison into our bloodstream that goes straight to our hearts. It will cause a clotting effect and thickening of our hearts and separate us from the things God deposited into us through His spirit.

There's no antidote for spiritual poison except repentance. Only the blood of Jesus Christ can counterattack the venom of bitterness and bring relief and healing. Still, it starts with us making the difficult decision to trust God and let go of our right to pass judgment on our enemies.

Once we choose to forgive our abusers of their sins against us, God can forgive us for our sins against Him.

I GOT BIT

When Suzanne and I returned home to south Louisiana after several years of youth pastoring, we took a break from full-time ministry. We had to let God heal some wounds we gained from our previous ministry experience.

We returned to our home church and enjoyed being church members for a change without the added responsibility of pastoring people. After a month, we started attending a small cell group, building relationships with new people, and re-establishing relationships with old friends.

One day, our small group leaders announced they were stepping down and moving away. They needed a new couple to step up and continue leading the group. No one wanted the responsibility, but since Suzanne and I had ministry experience, they encouraged us to fill in. After we prayed, we accepted the position and, within two weeks, became the new small group leaders.

Things were going well for about three weeks. Then I got a call from the Associate Pastor to address a complaint. Someone told him I was not following the laid-out structure for leading the small group. The structure plan calls for two worship songs at the beginning of class, but I directed our group into three songs instead of two. By doing this, I was extending the time limit and causing delays for everyone in the class.

I sat there and listened to this complaint and couldn't believe someone had complained about an extra worship song. The person who complained was the person who wrote out the class structure, and she perceived my action as an act of rebellion and disrespect to her authority.

I was stunned at being accused of these strong accusations. I was even more stunned that a complaint this small was being treated like I had led an insurrection against the whole church. The Associate Pastor decided to dismiss me as cell group leader.

There are no words to describe how furious that made me. I was so shocked and angry at such an extreme reaction over something I considered a small thing.

I could have chosen to apologize and agree to follow the structured plan, but this had gone beyond that. There was a bigger problem at work here, and I struggled to wrap my mind around it.

Yes, I confess, I took a solid offense to this decision. I knew who lodged this complaint against me. I became very bitter with her and the Associate Pastor for acting so petty and making a significant mountain out of a tiny molehill. This decision was not about an extra worship song; it felt more like a personal attack.

Every time I saw these individuals at church for two years, I turned and stormed in a different direction. I refused to talk to them or even offer a polite greeting. They didn't deserve my kindness. They needed to see my anger against them and then beg me to forgive them.

The poison of bitterness grew in my heart until I could no longer enter worship like I once did. My joy was dimming, and I was becoming short-tempered in my relationships at home and with other people.

Finally, one day during Sunday worship, God spoke directly to my heart and challenged me to go right then and repent for my anger against them. It became evident that the poison of my bitterness was directly responsible for my inability to worship and find peace from God.

I stood there in my spot and contemplated this challenge from God. If I do what He's challenging, I will feel better and free from this heaviness. If I don't, I'm choosing to disobey God and suffer even more consequences for my disobedience.

Reluctantly, I gave up the fight, excused myself away from Suzanne's side, and walked out the back of the sanctuary towards the office where I knew I would find the Associate Pastor.

When I arrived, I explained to him I needed to repent of my bitterness and then told him why. When he heard my confession, his eyes widened in shock as he remembered our conversation two years earlier. Then, he humbled himself and asked for MY forgiveness.

After our previous conversation, he learned that the accusations against me were not wholly accurate. He had set it in his heart to call me in once more and apologize to me for his actions, but he forgot. It completely slipped his mind to tell me he was wrong, and now he wanted to make things right between us.

Inside, I wanted to scream at him, "WHAT? You mean I could have saved myself two whole years of being furious at you for what you did, but you FORGOT to apologize to me?" But I restrained myself and responded in a polite Christian fashion.

We both agreed to forgive each other and declare the situation settled. Since I forgave him, I have had nothing but love for him, and we have maintained our friendship over the years.

After that conversation, I found my accuser and told her

the same thing I told him. She was very polite, accepted my apology, and told me she never knew anything was wrong between us.

I wanted to call her out, "WHAT? You mean we go to the same church, see each other every week, and I haven't talked to you for two years, and you didn't even notice something was wrong?" But again, I restrained myself and held my tongue.

It frustrated me that she never noticed how angry I was with her. I worked so hard to avoid her at church all this time, and she never even noticed. She didn't suffer one bit while I struggled each week to keep my distance from her.

I wanted to storm away and start avoiding her again so she'd notice this time. Still, I remember that I was there to resolve our differences, to be a peacemaker, and obey God, which is precisely what I did.

I later thought back on this and laughed at myself. It served as a perfect example of how our anger and bitterness against other people is no punishment against them. Still, we punish ourselves instead by fueling our bitterness against them. We are the ones who suffer from the poison of bitterness and unforgiveness, not them.

I forgave both of my offenders that day, and since then, I no longer feel bitter toward either of them. I still remember what happened, but I no longer hold it against them or try to pass judgment on them for what they did.

I was also free again to worship, and I felt a significant presence of God come over me and refresh me. It was so freeing to rid my life of the poison of bitterness.

17

HOW DO I KNOW IF I'VE FORGIVEN OR NOT?

"Have I forgiven them?" This is an honest question that I have asked myself many times. We pray and ask God to help us forgive our offenders, but we still struggle with unpleasant feelings and wonder if we forgave them. Did we? How do we know if we did or not?

I thought I had already dealt with my anger issues with my mother. Still, I became hardened and angry every year around Mother's Day. I HATED Mother's Day.

When my mother was alive, my family still expected me to show some sort of respectful appreciation to her for her efforts in mothering me. I would stand in the card section at Walmart, searching long and hard for the right card that didn't say "To the BEST Mother in the World" or "I'm so Grateful You're My Mother." Blech!

I got sick reading those mushy cards and became depressed because I never had a mother that fit that description. Why couldn't I find a card that read, "You gave me life; I got you this card. Call it even?"

The first Mother's Day after she passed away was such a

relief. I didn't have to go through the motions anymore, and I could focus all my attention on my wife, the BEST mother in the world.

Now, every year on Mother's Day weekend, I honor the memory of my mother by watching Faye Dunaway play Joan Crawford in *Mommie Dearest*. Oh, I can seriously relate to that movie. My wife always rolls her eyes and walks out of the room when it's on.

People sometimes question my dark sense of humor when I post on Facebook a Happy Mother's Day meme from Norman Bates or *Mommie Dearest*. They simply don't understand me.

These actions lead me to ask myself: Have I forgiven my mother? I know I prayed about forgiveness before, several times. I have laid it all out before God, weeping and praying for His help forgiving her.

And then, I realized I had all these unrealistic expectations about myself regarding forgiveness.

It's taken me years to learn that forgetting the abuse is not a part of forgiveness. I will never forget it. I know what happened, and I cannot deny that Mom was an abuser and I was a victim. That's not unforgiveness speaking; that's just declaring a fact. I'm not living in denial; it's a simple reality.

As I counsel others in forgiveness, I realize I'm not the only one who struggles with memories and occasional waves of emotion. Some days, I can talk about it and discuss it as a matter of fact with no difficulty. But there are other days when I think about it and find myself flooded with emotion. This display of emotion is not a sign of unforgiveness; it's just painful memories resurfacing in my mind.

Unforgiveness would be if I became angry and filled with

a growing desire to dig her back up and stomp her back into the ground six feet deeper.

I know, I know. Technically, we had Mom cremated, and she was sprinkled and not buried, but I think you know what I mean.

Now, whenever I think about her, I no longer feel angry. I just feel pity for myself that I never got to experience what it's like to have a loving mother in my life. I feel sorry for her because she was poisoned with bitterness and missed out on the joy life had to offer her.

Have you forgiven your offender? Do you still become angry whenever you hear his name in conversation? Do you still see that person in a room or Walmart and become overwhelmed with unkind and violent thoughts against the one who hurt you? If you do, I think it's safe to say you still struggle to forgive your offenders.

FORGIVING MY INSTRUCTOR

I had an instructor in Bible school, Tom, who was not very kind to me. Our personalities were like oil and vinegar; we simply did not blend well together. I felt I was being mistreated, but I wondered if I was too sensitive. Then other people around me started noticing it and checking on me out of love and concern. That confirmed that my suspicions were correct; he seriously didn't like me.

I almost quit school a few times but remembered that God brought me to that school of ministry. If God brought me to it, He would get me through it; so I stayed and endured Tom's mistreatment.

It was a challenging year, but I finally graduated, moved on, and became a youth pastor. Over the years, I harbored unpleasant feelings against Tom whenever someone mentioned his name in conversation or if I found myself in his presence. I recognized my feelings were turning to bitterness, so I brought this to God in prayer before the poison of bitterness overwhelmed me again.

In my studies, the Lord kept bringing me to Matthew 22.

> *A Pharisee asked Jesus, "What is the greatest commandment in the Law?" Jesus replied: " 'Love the Lord your God with all your heart and with all your soul and with all your mind.' This is the first and greatest commandment. And the second is like it: 'Love your neighbor as yourself.' All the Law and the Prophets hang on these two commandments." (Matthew 22:36-40)*

Every time I read that, I am reminded of the second commandment. I already got the first one down. It's easy. It's always easy to love someone who loves you in return. But that second commandment isn't as easy as the first. Some people are just difficult to love. In fact, for some people, it seems downright impossible.

Reading that scripture challenged me to examine my relationship with my instructor and ask myself, "Do I really love him?"

I started praying and asking God to help me forgive this man who made my year in Bible school so difficult. I honestly poured my heart out to God and started praying for God to bless him, his family, and his ministry.

One day, I tested my ability to forgive by calling him. I wanted to see if I could have a friendly conversation without the ill feelings coming back to my heart against him.

I looked up his number, dialed it, took a deep breath, and waited for him to answer.

"Hello?" It was him.

"Hey, Tom, this is Scott."

"Scott Green?" he questioned.

"Yeah, it's me. How are you doing?"

"How did you get my number?" I didn't expect that response, and I could hear the tone of his voice drop. He was not happy to hear from me.

"I looked you up. It's not that hard to do. I wanted to reach out to you and see how you're doing. It's been a long time."

His tone changed again and became very cold, sharp, and matter-of-fact. "Oh well, you know, we're just going and blowing." And then silence. He didn't even return the same courtesy by asking how I was doing, just awkward silence.

I quickly made an excuse to end the conversation because I could tell this was going nowhere. After I hung up, I was fuming with rage all over again. That's it; I'm done. I'm not trying anymore. I was angrier than before because I actually tried. I don't need him if Tom doesn't want to be my friend either.

THE GIFT OFFERING

Over time, I noticed my attitude regarding Tom, my instructor, getting worse and worse. My worship of God was becoming increasingly complex, and I remembered my previous experience with bitterness against the Associate Pastor.

"Lord? How am I supposed to love someone I don't even LIKE?" Then the Lord brought a scripture to my memory:

Therefore, if you are offering your gift at the altar and remember that your brother or sister has something against you, leave your gift there in front of the altar. First go and be reconciled to them; then come and offer your gift to me. (Matthew 5:23-24)

Wow, it was all becoming very clear to me. Whenever we worship the Lord in church, we give Him our gift offering of worship and praise. But what happens if God refuses our offering of praise? What if He looked at us and said, "Stop, put that gift down; I don't want it."

"Why, God? Why would You reject my sacrifice of praise?"

"Because it's tainted."

"Tainted? How? Did I do something wrong?"

"What is the greatest commandment in My Word?"

"I remember this one. It's in Matthew 22. Love the Lord your God with all your heart and with all your soul and with all your mind. I already do, Lord. That's why I'm here, to offer You my heart in praise and worship."

"And what is the second greatest commandment?"

"Love my neighbor as myself."

"Yes, and what does My Word say about the second greatest commandment?"

"Um...let me think. It says the second is like the first, and all the Law and the prophets hang on these two commandments."

"That's correct. That means loving one another is just as important as loving Me with all your heart."

"You mean..."

"Yes, as long as you have bitterness in your heart, then

your offering of praise to Me is tainted with the poison of bitterness. I cannot accept that kind of offering."

"So, what do I need to do for You to accept my offerings?"

"Put your gift down at the altar. Then go to your offender and forgive him. Once you do this, you may return to the altar here and then offer your gift of praise to Me, and I will accept it."

This entire conversation reminds me of God's conversation with another one of His children, who struggled with jealousy and anger towards his brother.

> *"Now Abel kept flocks, and Cain worked the soil. In the course of time Cain brought some of the fruits of the soil as an offering to the Lord. And Abel also brought an offering—fat portions from some of the firstborn of his flock. The Lord looked with favor on Abel and his offering, but on Cain and his offering he did not look with favor. So Cain was very angry, and his face was downcast. Then the Lord said to Cain, "Why are you angry? Why is your face downcast? If you do what is right, will you not be accepted?" (Genesis 4:2-6)*

Cain had deep anger and jealousy issues against his brother Abel. He always felt inferior and jealous of God's favor for his brother. God could not accept his offering as long as Cain held these grudges and bitterness against Abel. It was tainted.

As long as we hold on to bitterness, anger, unforgiveness, or grudges, God will continue to reject our offering, no matter what we bring to Him.

How can we love God with all our hearts but not His people? We can't. The nature of God IS His people. My immediate response was, "But, God, have you SEEN how some of these people treat others? They're not the easiest people in the world to love."

"Neither were the people who crucified Me, but I forgave them."

"Come on. Really? Are you going to play that card on me again? You KNOW I can't come back with anything now." Yes, sometimes, this is how God and I communicate with each other.

Then He reminded me: *"If you love me, keep my commands." (John 14:15)*

"But what if I try to make peace with Tom and he doesn't accept it?"

"If anyone will not welcome you or listen to your words, leave that home or town and shake the dust off your feet. Truly I tell you, it will be more bearable for Sodom and Gomorrah on the day of judgment than for that town." (Matthew 10:14-15)

"Ahhhh, I get it. So as long as I forgive my offender and offer the olive branch of peace between us, that's all I can do. If Tom rejects my forgiveness, then the responsibility is no longer mine to bear. Is that right?"

"Correct, and he will become My responsibility to judge, not yours."

"I'm sorry, Lord. Please forgive me for holding on to these offenses."

"I forgive you. But now you need to forgive your offender."

"Right away, Lord."

Dang, I can't argue that with God. He has an answer for everything. I can complain all day long, but the Holy Spirit keeps bringing me back to this. The challenge is right in front of me. I will have to swallow my stinking pride and forgive this man. So I prayed, and I prayed hard.

THE REUNION

It wasn't long after this challenge from God that I received an invitation to our Bible School Reunion. I was eager to return and reunite with old friends, but I also knew I would face Tom again. "Oh great, I suppose you knew this was coming, didn't you, Lord? I guess this is where I'm supposed to approach Tom and tell him I forgive him, right?" God didn't respond this time.

I prepared to go to that reunion and face Tom if the opportunity presented itself. Yes, I said IF. I was trying to justify not going through with it.

As I prayed, I told God that if the opportunity didn't present itself naturally, I would take that as a sign to leave it alone. So I went to the reunion and stayed alert to any supernatural opportunity.

At the beginning of the evening, I walked through the door and saw Tom; we crossed paths immediately. We exchanged empty but polite pleasantries and then parted in different directions. That was not a good opportunity.

We mingled with old friends and enjoyed the reunion and service throughout the night, but we kept our distance. Still, no suitable opportunity presented itself. "Okay, Lord, I'm paying attention, but it isn't happening. Maybe I should drop it and let it go." Still, no response from God.

The night was drawing to a close, and I saw Tom get up from his seat, walk out of the sanctuary before the reunion was over, and walk into the church foyer alone. Dang, this is the excellent opportunity I was hoping to avoid. I took a deep breath and followed him outside.

Once I found Tom in the foyer, I approached him and began a casual conversation with him. Since I had already gained the courage to approach him alone, I was now determined to do what I set out to do.

After a few more polite pleasantries, I directed the conversation to my year under his leadership in Bible School. I confessed that I struggled through the entire year and then told him why. I held him accountable for everything he did to me as I recapped his actions and how they made me feel.

Tom sat silently, surprised that I would do this right now and there. I remained very calm and respectful, never raised my voice once, but maintained a proper tone and complete self-control. Still, I expressed to him that his treatment against me was hurtful and toxic, and I gave details to support my case.

Then I told Tom I was not here to create more conflict but to look him in the eye after all these years and finally say, "I forgive you!"

When I heard those words come out of my mouth, I suddenly felt powerful and courageous. I felt like I had just regained control of my life regarding Tom and our feud. It was like a wave of peace sweeping over me. I finally faced and confronted one of my offenders, held him accountable for his actions, and was strong enough to say, "I forgive you."

Tom didn't know what to say. After he collected his thoughts, he finally confessed to me that those early years of his leadership were toxic. God had already been dealing with him on several poor choices he had made. Tom also shared that he never realized he made me feel that way and was very sorry.

Bingo. I came tonight ready to tell my offender, "I forgive you," even though he hasn't asked for it. God dealt with my heart to reach out again and offer the olive branch of peace between us. I have learned that forgiveness doesn't excuse our abuse or offenses, and it's okay to hold our offenders accountable for their actions.

Thankfully, this had a happy ending. When it was all said and done, I went my way and never felt hostile or angry against Tom again. I can still remember what he did and how it made me feel. Whenever I speak of those days, I'm reminded by God that I already forgave him. I learned from this experience and a few similar ones that THIS is God's command to show love.

Forgiveness is not a feeling. We choose to put our pains and wounds aside and forgive, even if our offenders don't ask for it. We choose to forgive even if we are still hurting and struggling with the consequences of their abuse.

I chose that night to forgive Tom, and I meant it. My heart feels lighter, and my peace has returned, and THAT is how I know I forgave him, my sister, and ultimately my mother.

I can think back and remember all the pain and abuse I've experienced from my abusers, and while I will never forget, I have let go of my right to pass judgment on them. I gave it to God; it's gone. It's HIS responsibility now to deal with these individuals. I can now share my story without feeling the sting.

18

WHAT IF I AM THE OFFENDER?

It happens. No one is exempt from it. Sometimes, we all open our mouths, stick our feet in, and choke on our words. Either it came out all wrong, or we said a bad thing at the wrong time, and someone took offense to what we said. How often do we wish we could go back in time and undo something we said or did?

You've done it. I've done it, maybe more times than you have, but I certainly have done my share of eating crow. Sometimes I'm unaware that I said or did anything that someone else took offense to. I mean no harm, but sometimes I do not carefully choose my words or consider my audience.

I was preaching once about how people spend more money pimping their cell phones and cars than they spend on missions. It was an excellent point; several people responded with a firm "Amen."

As soon as the service was over, I got a severe tongue lashing from an older gentleman who took great offense at me using the term *pimping* in service. No amount of explaining myself would satisfy him, so I simply humbled myself, thanked him for correcting me, and promised to do my best never to repeat that term.

As a pastor, several offended people have approached me, ready to share what I said or did that offended them. Sometimes, when certain people step up with that particular look, I already know what they are about to say. I want to look at them and respond with, "WHAT? What did I do THIS time?" Then I brace myself for the scathing report.

Some people seem to be on a witch hunt, just looking to take offense at every little thing.

Sometimes, the report is so silly that I cannot help but snicker that someone took offense to it. Take, for example, me leading an extra song of worship instead of the written-in-stone by God's holy finger TWO-song structure for small groups.

I lost a church member once because I mispronounced proper Biblical names and geographical locations. According to them, I didn't find the appropriate pronunciation of the Old Testament names important enough to study and practice how to say them correctly.

I was too busy focusing on other points of my message and teaching the fundamentals of LOVING ONE ANOTHER to worry about saying a name correctly or not. As soon as I mispronounced a name or location, she would stand up and walk out of church until she finally stopped coming.

I have a memory that comes to mind of an old skit Steve Martin used to do on *Saturday Night Live* on TV. Whenever he did or said something that offended someone, he would speak in a very sarcastic tone, "Well, excuuuuuuse meeeeeee!"

Yes, I confess, sometimes, when confronted with some of these immaterial offenses, I replay that memory in my mind's eye. I can hear it in the back of my head while trying to maintain a proper and dignified attitude in front of them.

"Oh, I'm sorry, did I pronounce his name wrong again? Well, excuuuuuuuse meeeeee!"

"What? Did it offend you because I greeted your sister before church and didn't greet you? Well excuuuuuuuuse meeeeeeeeee!"

Sure, some of their offenses are silly and immaterial to us. Yes, some people need to get over themselves and stop getting offended at every little thing. But when people approach us with an offense, we still have a Christian responsibility to hear that person out respectfully and consider their complaint.

PERCEPTIONS

I had a woman come to me once after church, and she was hopping mad. I saw her coming and instantly knew this would be an unpleasant confrontation. This very opinionated woman loved Jesus, but she also loved being brutally honest with people. She felt her duty was to inform you of everything you were doing wrong so you could become a better person. She said it was one of her spiritual gifts.

When she came to me, she reported that someone highly offended her. Another woman in our church who grew tired of her constant complaining called her out and accused her of being rude. Can you imagine that?

"I don't have to stand here and let this woman call me rude in church. I've never been rude to her. She should know I was only trying to help her. If this is how I will be treated, I can find another church where people don't accuse me of being something I'm not." I fought hard not to roll my eyes or let my frustration reflect on my face.

Suddenly, inspiration hit me out of nowhere. "Well, even if what the lady said is not true, SOMETHING you did gave her that impression about you. She was sharing with you her honest perspective on your behavior. Instead of getting offended, why don't you stop for a moment and ask yourself what you did to give her that impression." Ask yourself, 'Why does she think this about me?' If you can discover what you did to give her that wrong perception, perhaps you can work on changing that perception, proving she's wrong, instead of just taking offense and leaving?"

She gazed at me blankly, and then her face lit up as if a light bulb had gone off in her head. "That's it!" She said, "I'll work on changing her perception of me and let her get to know the real me."

When she walked away, I could hold it back no longer. I finally rolled my eyes, took a deep breath, and walked back to my office, proud of myself for that inspired stroke of wisdom, and thought, "God, we should charge extra for that."

That experience has stuck with me. Even though I find some people's offenses against me to be trite and immaterial, God instructs us to be peacekeepers. I must always show respect when listening to a complaint and ask myself, "WHY do they have this perception of me?" "What did I do to create this impression they have on me or my character?" "What would it take for me to correct this perception?"

Even if I disagree with their perception of my actions or motives, it's not my job to defend myself constantly. I shouldn't pass their complaints off as petty or silly.

Instead, it's my job as a Christian to hear them out and

examine myself to see if I did anything to deserve that complaint. And if that's what they think about me, then I need to work harder to change that perception.

If I offended someone, I should accept corrections, consider my ways and make every effort not to offend that individual again.

> *Make every effort to live in peace with everyone and to be holy; without holiness no one will see the Lord. See to it that no one falls short of the grace of God and that no bitter root grows up to cause trouble and defile many.*
> *(Hebrews 12:14-15)*

A CRACKED POT

Imagine the most beautiful handmade flowerpot you ever saw. The flowerpot was painted by an aspiring artist whose pieces have become quite valuable to art collectors worldwide, and you own it.

Imagine that the flowerpot fell and broke into several pieces by accident. Your prized art piece is now worthless and damaged. Even though it has now lost its monetary value, you still love the pot. You can't seem to part with it, so you purchase the strongest glue and carefully glue the pieces back together.

It isn't perfect, but at least it's back together. Upon examination, you can make out the cracks; but you decide it still has personal value, and you plant fresh flowers in it.

Every time you look at the pot, you see the cracks, reminding you of that terrible day your flowerpot broke. The crevices and gaps along the sides and edges are a constant reminder of how you felt when you found it broken. But, you don't care anymore because you can still enjoy it for its beauty and renewed usefulness to bed your prize-winning flowers.

We are like that beautiful flowerpot. A perfect artist created us to reflect and display His beautiful glory, but somehow we became broken. We felt shattered and worthless, but at our lowest moment God picked up our broken pieces and put us back together again.

We may still have some cracks and scars that remind us of our brokenness, but we are still just as beautiful and valuable to our creator.

God desires to use your cracks and scars to testify how His healing can repair any brokenness in your life.

I recognize I am a cracked pot. My scars and cracks remind me every day of my brokenness. My scars will never go away, but that doesn't make me worthless or any less beautiful in God's eyes. My scars and brokenness now serve as a constant reminder and testimony of how God healed me. It all began with my decision to offer forgiveness to my abusers.

I am no longer living my life as a victim of my past. I am free. There's no more hiding and no more secrets.

IN CLOSING

Wow, what an emotional journey through forgiveness this has been! I know it brought back some uncomfortable emotions and memories I haven't revisited in a while. It also served as a refresher of what God taught me and reminded me of the testimony of my scars.

I am stronger because of what I experienced and have gained strength, wisdom, and healing. I hope and pray for you to experience similar victories in your life after taking this journey of forgiveness with me.

Please don't wait until it stops hurting to forgive. Don't let your feelings dictate your actions, and don't fall for the unrealistic expectations that forgiveness requires immediate trust and reconciliation on your part. It's okay to draw boundaries and separate yourself from your abusers if they refuse to take responsibility for abusing you.

But it's NOT okay to allow the poison of bitterness to pollute your bloodstream and harden your heart from the glorious things God has in store for you.

No amount of vengeful acts you can bring against your abuser can measure up to what God can do if you just give it to Him and let Him have it.

I will leave you with a proclamation. It's the same proclamation I speak over my new grandson Jackson whenever I see him. By proclaiming this over him, I believe I am speaking these things into his life, and now I will also declare them into your life. You are strong, you are smart, and you are loved.

IF YOU NEED HELP

If you or anyone you know is a victim of physical or sexual abuse, please call The National Domestic Hotline at 1 (800) 799-7233. They are available 24/7 and ready to assist.

You can also contact TheHotline.org and begin a chat with a live operator. It's free and confidential.

ACKNOWLEDGMENTS

I would like to acknowledge the following people for the inspiration and input they had in my life...

My father, Ray Green, *Thank you for believing in me. You will always be my "Champ".*

Pastor Jeff Ables and Pastor Joe Cormier, *My two pastors who offered love, encouragement and spiritual guidance along my journey of forgiveness.*

Tammy Debose, *Thank you for your love and support and for being like a sister to me over the years.*

Special Thank You to: *Seth & Jackson Griffin, Mary Teresa Dennis, Margaret Kresse, Shawn & Nichole Marcell, Carroll & Bea Latiolais, and Sudie Landry. It's the little things you do that make me Smile, Laugh, and Love Life a little more. Thank you for being there when I needed your friendship and love.*

My Mother and Sister:
I Forgive You!

ABOUT THE AUTHOR

Scott Green has been a Certified Minister for 30 years. He graduated from Ministry Training College in 1992 and has been in active full-time ministry as a Youth Minister, Associate Pastor, and Senior Pastor for over 20 years.

Scott was a victim of physical, mental, and sexual abuse as a child and young adult. He has learned firsthand the struggles of healing and forgiveness and has shared his experience and lessons in his first book: *70 x 7*.

Scott lives in south Louisiana with his beautiful wife of 30 years and has two beautiful daughters, a handsome son-in-law and one handsome grandson. He enjoys writing, preaching, and part-time acting in television and movies.

If you enjoyed reading this book, please consider leaving a review on Amazon. Each review helps new readers discover my book. Thank You.

Contact: 70x7book@gmail.com

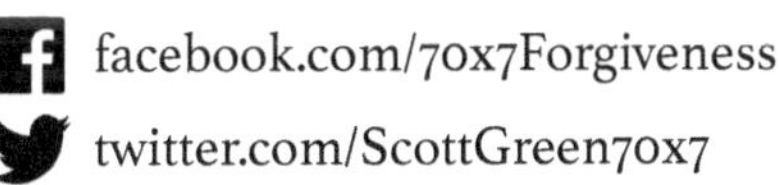